Understanding How Students Develop

WITHDRAWN
From the
Mishawaka-Penn
Harris Public
Library

PRACTICAL GUIDES FOR LIBRARIANS

About the Series

This innovative series written and edited for librarians by librarians provides authoritative, practical information and guidance on a wide spectrum of library processes and operations.

Books in the series are focused, describing practical and innovative solutions to a problem facing today's librarian and delivering step-by-step guidance for planning, creating, implementing, managing, and evaluating a wide range of services and programs.

The books are aimed at beginning and intermediate librarians needing basic instruction/guidance in a specific subject and at experienced librarians who need to gain knowledge in a new area or guidance in implementing a new program/service.

About the Series Editor

The **Practical Guides for Librarians** series was conceived by and is edited by M. Sandra Wood, MLS, MBA, AHIP, FMLA, Librarian Emerita, Penn State University Libraries.

M. Sandra Wood was a librarian at the George T. Harrell Library, the Milton S. Hershey Medical Center, College of Medicine, Pennsylvania State University, Hershey, PA, for over thirty-five years, specializing in reference, educational, and database services. Ms. Wood worked for several years as a development editor for Neal-Schuman Publishers.

Ms. Wood received an MLS from Indiana University and an MBA from the University of Maryland. She is a fellow of the Medical Library Association and served as a member of MLA's Board of Directors from 1991 to 1995. Ms. Wood is founding and current editor of *Medical Reference Services Quarterly*, now in its thirty-fifth volume. She also was founding editor of the *Journal of Consumer Health on the Internet* and the *Journal of Electronic Resources in Medical Libraries* and served as editor/coeditor of both journals through 2011.

Titles in the Series

1. *How to Teach: A Practical Guide for Librarians* by Beverley E. Crane
2. *Implementing an Inclusive Staffing Model for Today's Reference Services* by Julia K. Nims, Paula Storm, and Robert Stevens
3. *Managing Digital Audiovisual Resources: A Practical Guide for Librarians* by Matthew C. Mariner
4. *Outsourcing Technology: A Practical Guide for Librarians* by Robin Hastings
5. *Making the Library Accessible for All: A Practical Guide for Librarians* by Jane Vincent

6. *Discovering and Using Historical Geographic Resources on the Web: A Practical Guide for Librarians* by Eva H. Dodsworth and L. W. Laliberté
7. *Digitization and Digital Archiving: A Practical Guide for Librarians* by Elizabeth R. Leggett
8. *Makerspaces: A Practical Guide for Librarians* by John J. Burke
9. *Implementing Web-Scale Discovery Services: A Practical Guide for Librarians* by JoLinda Thompson
10. *Using iPhones and iPads: A Practical Guide for Librarians* by Matthew Connolly and Tony Cosgrave
11. *Usability Testing: A Practical Guide for Librarians* by Rebecca Blakiston
12. *Mobile Devices: A Practical Guide for Librarians* by Ben Rawlins
13. *Going Beyond Loaning Books to Loaning Technologies: A Practical Guide for Librarians* by Janelle Sander, Lori S. Mestre, and Eric Kurt
14. *Children's Services Today: A Practical Guide for Librarians* by Jeanette Larson
15. *Genealogy: A Practical Guide for Librarians* by Katherine Pennavaria
16. *Collection Evaluation in Academic Libraries: A Practical Guide for Librarians* by Karen C. Kohn
17. *Creating Online Tutorials: A Practical Guide for Librarians* by Hannah Gascho Rempel and Maribeth Slebodnik
18. *Using Google Earth in Libraries: A Practical Guide for Librarians* by Eva Dodsworth and Andrew Nicholson
19. *Integrating the Web into Everyday Library Services: A Practical Guide for Librarians* by Elizabeth R. Leggett
20. *Infographics: A Practical Guide for Librarians* by Beverley E. Crane
21. *Meeting Community Needs: A Practical Guide for Librarians* by Pamela H. MacKellar
22. *3D Printing: A Practical Guide for Librarians* by Sara Russell Gonzalez and Denise Beaubien Bennett
23. *Patron-Driven Acquisitions in Academic and Special Libraries: A Practical Guide for Librarians* by Steven Carrico, Michelle Leonard, and Erin Gallagher
24. *Collaborative Grant-Seeking: A Practical Guide for Librarians* by Bess G. de Farber
25. *Story-Time Success: A Practical Guide for Librarians* by Katie Fitzgerald
26. *Teaching Google Scholar: A Practical Guide for Librarians* by Paige Alfonzo
27. *Teen Services Today: A Practical Guide for Librarians* by Sara K. Joiner and Geri Swanzy
28. *Data Management: A Practical Guide for Librarians* by Margaret E. Henderson
29. *Online Teaching and Learning: A Practical Guide for Librarians* by Beverley E. Crane
30. *Writing Effectively in Print and on the Web: A Practical Guide for Librarians* by Rebecca Blakiston
31. *Gamification: A Practical Guide for Librarians* by Elizabeth McMunn-Tetangco
32. *Providing Reference Services: A Practical Guide for Librarians* by John Gottfried and Katherine Pennavaria
33. *Video Marketing for Libraries: A Practical Guide for Librarians* by Heather A. Dalal, Robin O'Hanlan, and Karen Yacobucci
34. *Understanding How Students Develop: A Practical Guide for Librarians* by Hannah Gascho Rempel, Kelly McElroy, and Laurie M. Bridges

Understanding How Students Develop

A Practical Guide for Librarians

Hannah Gascho Rempel

Kelly McElroy

Laurie M. Bridges

PRACTICAL GUIDES FOR LIBRARIANS, NO. 34

Property of
Mishawaka-Penn-Harris
Public Library
Mishawaka, Indiana

ROWMAN & LITTLEFIELD
Lanham • Boulder • New York • London

Published by Rowman & Littlefield
A wholly owned subsidiary of The Rowman & Littlefield Publishing Group, Inc.
4501 Forbes Boulevard, Suite 200, Lanham, Maryland 20706
www.rowman.com

Unit A, Whitacre Mews, 26-34 Stannary Street, London SE11 4AB

Copyright © 2017 by Rowman & Littlefield

All rights reserved. No part of this book may be reproduced in any form or by any electronic or mechanical means, including information storage and retrieval systems, without written permission from the publisher, except by a reviewer who may quote passages in a review.

British Library Cataloguing in Publication Information Available

Library of Congress Cataloging-in-Publication Data

Names: Rempel, Hannah Gascho, author. | McElroy, Kelly, author. | Bridges, Laurie M., 1972– author.
Title: Understanding how students develop : a practical guide for librarians / Hannah Gascho Rempel, Kelly McElroy, Laurie M. Bridges.
Description: Lanham, Maryland : Rowman & Littlefield, 2017. | Series: Practical guides for librarians ; 34 | Includes bibliographical references and index.
Identifiers: LCCN 2017013078 (print) | LCCN 2017028702 (ebook) | ISBN 9781442279223 (electronic) | ISBN 9781442279216 (pbk. : alk. paper)
Subjects: LCSH: Libraries and education. | Learning, Psychology of. | Educational psychology.
Classification: LCC Z718 (ebook) | LCC Z718 .R46 2017 (print) | DDC 021.2/4—dc23
LC record available at https://lccn.loc.gov/2017013078

∞™ The paper used in this publication meets the minimum requirements of American National Standard for Information Sciences—Permanence of Paper for Printed Library Materials, ANSI/NISO Z39.48-1992.

Printed in the United States of America

Contents

List of Figures and Tables		ix
Preface		xi
Acknowledgments		xv
Chapter 1	**Turning Theory into Practice**	1
Chapter 2	**Encouraging Intellectual Growth**	19
Chapter 3	**Making Sense of Difficult Problems**	41
Chapter 4	**Building on Past Learning Experiences**	55
Chapter 5	**Developing the Learner's Voice**	67
Chapter 6	**Understanding How Sense of Self Changes over Time**	79
Chapter 7	**Engaging Learners in Their Education**	101
Chapter 8	**Connecting Current and Future Theories**	115
Appendix: Further Recommended Reading		131
Index		133
About the Authors		135

Figures and Tables

Figures

Figure 1.1. How theories are developed	3
Figure 1.2. Four possible uses for theory	6
Figure 1.3. Student development theories and influencing factors	14
Figure 2.1. Intellectual development phases by typical age range	22
Figure 2.2. Intellectual development transition points	24
Figure 3.1. Reflective Judgment Model phases of thinking	43
Figure 3.2. An iterative question-based approach	50
Figure 5.1. Growth in self-authoring	69
Figure 5.2. Learning Partnerships Model	70
Figure 6.1. The eight ages of man, Erik Erikson, 1963	81
Figure 6.2. Developing competence	82
Figure 6.3. Managing emotions	85
Figure 6.4. Moving through autonomy toward interdependence	87
Figure 6.5. Developing mature interpersonal relationships	89
Figure 6.6. Establishing identity	91
Figure 6.7. Developing purpose	93
Figure 6.8. Developing integrity	94

Figure 7.1. Frequency of "student engagement" and "student involvement" — 104

Figure 7.2. Recommendation area for the youth section — 111

Figure 7.3. Engagement processes in reading framework — 111

Figure 8.1. Theory-to-Practice Model — 123

Tables

Table 1.1. Characteristics of theories and common sense — 5

Table 1.2. Example of using theory as a guide for setting goals — 8

Table 1.3. Examples of individual reflective practices — 10

Table 2.1. Suggested source types based on intellectual development phase — 28

Table 2.2. Research consultation prompts — 29

Table 2.3. Instructional strategies for library sessions — 33

Table 4.1. Epistemological Reflection Model gender patterns — 58

Table 4.2. Tutoring techniques that encourage shared problem solving — 61

Table 4.3. Multiple viewpoints note-taking guide — 64

Table 5.1. Audience analysis exercise sample handout — 75

Table 6.1. Developing competence in a library setting — 83

Table 6.2. Managing emotions in a library setting — 86

Table 6.3. Moving through autonomy toward interdependence in a library setting — 88

Table 6.4. Developing mature interpersonal relationships in a library setting — 90

Table 6.5. Suggestions for reflective listening — 96

Table 8.1. Summary of student development theories — 117

Table 8.2. Summary of suggested library practices based on student development theories — 118

Table 8.3. Comparing programmatic guiding statements over time — 127

Preface

Why Should You Read a Book on Student Development Theories?

Librarians connect people with information. To achieve these connections librarians carefully craft collections to meet their learners' needs; they design instructional experiences to help learners deal with an ever-changing information landscape; and they seek to preserve information and make that information findable for future learners. To find out if and how learners are using information, librarians routinely perform usability tests, track circulation figures, and keep pace with the latest technological trends their learners' adopt. These forms of evaluation allow librarians to become more informed about their overall learner population. But librarians rarely receive training on how to address the individual needs of their learners, especially training that explores how intellectual development, identity development, and ways of engaging in a community shape how learners interact with information at different points of their lives.

A deeper understanding of learners' development makes it easier to see the world through different lenses and to act with more empathy. The field of student development theories provides insight and inspiration for librarians seeking to better understand the struggles learners sometimes have when faced with new information and provides ways to think about learners' interactions with information as extending beyond considerations of their academic capabilities. Development theories recognize that learners who are questioning their identity and are seeking increasing independence, or who are seeking authentic connections within their community, may need different types of information-need supports.

Librarians work with learners across their life-span, in academic settings and other communities that are increasingly diverse. The wider range of experiences that both learners and librarians bring to information-driven questions calls for a more nuanced understanding of learners' development so that librarians can present relevant opportunities for learners to engage with information. Throughout *Understanding How Students Develop: A Practical Guide for Librarians*, examples of how development theories can be used in reference, outreach, and instruction will be presented to help facilitate a practical understanding of the range of types of development. Hopefully, these examples will spark your thinking so that you can both learn more about the theories behind learner development and adapt the examples to your own context.

What Can Librarians Learn from the Field of Student Affairs?

Student development theories grew out of the field of student affairs. Student affairs offices are a common fixture on U.S. college campuses. The field of student affairs focuses on student activities outside of the classroom and can include professionals working in such areas as recreational sports, student advising, counseling and mental health, student health services, residential life, career services, and international studies. While the day-to-day work of librarians and student affairs professionals is not the same, the way librarians and student affairs professionals interact with learners, especially in academic settings, has many similarities. Librarians tend to work with learners outside of the classroom and are not typically responsible for giving students grades (although some librarians do teach credit courses). Like many counselors and advisors, librarians work with learners one-on-one through reference consultations. Student affairs professionals offer guest lecturers and plan programs and outreach events—activities that many librarians also carry out on a regular basis.

Unlike student affairs professionals such as advisors, who are only able to hold consultations with students for a limited time due to the high volume of students they serve, librarians often have the flexibility to spend more time with learners working through their information questions. As a result, librarians can sometimes build meaningful connections with learners that reveal struggles learners are having with their classes, instructors, or with the larger institution. Recognizing how these challenges relate to student development theories can provide librarians with a framework for giving supportive and safe challenges to students.

Student development theories have grown out of the observations and practical work of student affairs professionals since the 1950s. Many learners, across many institutions, were interviewed and surveyed as these theories were developed. Consequently, these theories help to describe the behaviors of a wide range of learners. However, it was not until recently that these theories began to take into account differences such as sexual orientation, socioeconomic status, and race. Some of these drawbacks will be discussed throughout *Understanding How Students Develop: A Practical Guide for Librarians*, and the field of student development theories is continuously seeking out ways to make their work relevant to a wider range of learners. However, just as librarians and information scientists still use information-seeking models while simultaneously reexamining their application in new settings, the basic framework of student development theories continues to give helpful strategies for better understanding learners.

What Theories Are Covered?

Understanding How Students Develop: A Practical Guide for Librarians will discuss seven main student development theories. The theories chosen represent some of the most established theories in the field. The theories chosen also represent a range of factors that influence learners at many life stages, including the way thinking and reasoning (or intellect) develops over time and how students' sense of self or identity changes. Most importantly, these theories were chosen because of their relevance to the work many librarians do as they interact with learners. Some of these theories actually have the word "theory" in their name. Other theories are called "models," and a few are referred to as "principles." In some disciplines, there is a clear line between these terms, but in the student development field, many of these terms are used interchangeably, and that approach will be used throughout this book. Here is a summary of the topics covered:

Chapter 1 provides a foundation for reading and applying theories to your practice. Understanding the role of theory in the work of practicing librarians will give strategies for integrating a range of theories into your work.

Chapters 2, 3, and 4 discuss three key intellectual or cognitive development theories: Perry's Intellectual and Ethical Development Theory, the Reflective Judgment Model, and the Epistemological Reflection Model. These theories explore how learners make meaning from information based on their developmental stage; how learners deal with complicated, authentic problems throughout their lives; and how learners' unique background experiences influence the way they process and interact with information.

Chapter 5 covers the Learning Partnerships Model, which is a theory that bridges intellectual and identity development theories. This theory discusses how learning environments can be constructed to support learners as they develop their own voices.

Chapter 6 discusses Identity Development Theory and explores the important role emotional and identity growth plays in how learners approach information and suggests approaches for creating safe environments for all learners.

Chapter 7 presents Student Involvement Theory, which suggests that learners who have many engagement opportunities and who are encouraged to engage in ways that are meaningful for them may be more successful as they face challenging transition phases in their lives.

Chapter 8 explores the ways these theories can be used in an integrative approach. In addition, gaps and future directions for the field of student development theories are addressed, along with suggestions for assessing the use of theories in practice. The appendix offers a list of recommended readings in the field of student development theories if you would like to continue your exploration.

What Is Practical about Theory?

What is a book on theory doing in a practical series? Reading about theories provides an opportunity to be more reflective and intentional about your work. Critically engaging with your work and asking questions that relate to your context will create opportunities for making authentic adjustments to your work that will be more meaningful than simply trying to stitch together a series of suggested practical tips. To that end, there are several objectives for this book:

- To guide you in understanding the role of theory in practice
- To help you engage with the concept that learners are more than just a sum of their academic histories but are also influenced by intellectual and identity development
- To introduce you to concrete ideas based on theories you can borrow or adapt to spark your practice

Understanding How Students Develop: A Practical Guide for Librarians does not suggest magical fixes for working with learners. People rarely behave and develop in easy or linear ways, and development models are not a recipe for success. But engaging with theories can provide you with a flexible toolkit as you seek new ways to connect learners with information.

Acknowledgments

We have many people to be thankful for—colleagues and friends who have shaped our thinking and have provided us with new perspectives as we continue to be lifelong learners. In particular, we would like to thank the College Student Services Administration program and the Student Affairs Division at Oregon State University for modeling student development theories in their practice on our campus. We are also thankful for the influence of our fellow teaching librarians—at our institution and beyond—especially those librarians (both named and anonymous) who allowed us to share their stories throughout this book. Finally, we would like to thank Lindy Brown, our colleague at Corvallis-Benton County Public Library, who provided many of the initial idea sparks for this book.

CHAPTER 1

Turning Theory into Practice

IN THIS CHAPTER

▷ Understanding how theories are developed and used

▷ Incorporating theories into library practice

▷ Introducing student development theories

HAVE YOU EVER THOUGHT ABOUT WHY YOU wash your hands before eating? Or why roses are more expensive at Valentine's Day? You probably have, and even if you don't have expertise in biology or economics, you are likely aware that larger frameworks inform these decisions. Those larger frameworks are called theories, and while you may not know the specific names of the theories behind these everyday behaviors, the choices to wash hands and increase prices are connected to theories. The recommendations for modern-day handwashing practices are the result of the development of germ theory. And the principles of supply and demand indicate that when something is in high demand, the price will likely go up and thus inform purchasing decisions. These are examples of theories that affect everyday practices such as maintaining your health and the way finances are managed.

Theories also affect librarians' day-to-day practices. A common library instruction goal is for learners to feel more comfortable asking a librarian for help. This goal is an outgrowth of the theory of library anxiety. Another example is the use of finger-play activities in children's story times; this practice draws on theories about the impact of play and movement on children's ability to learn. Similarly, theories about classification and order have influenced catalogers' decisions about what category or class a book should go into.

You may not consciously reflect on the theories you use in your everyday work, and few people turn to a textbook looking for a theory to help them make a decision about how to proceed with their day's activities. But having a broader understanding of theories can provide tools so you can be more strategic, systematic, and above all, more empathetic as you create programs and look for new ways to improve the work you do. It is often difficult to understand or imagine how people who are different from you learn, feel, or think. Differences between you and the people you work with may be a result of age, race, gender, sexual orientation, socioeconomic status, educational background, nation of origin, or a host of other experiences that make people unique. The value of theories is that they are typically based on a broad range of experiences, which are then distilled into a summary of that wider set of experiences. As a result, becoming familiar with theory can allow you to see through a variety of lenses and develop an understanding of the needs of people who are different from you.

Theories can serve as a guide for understanding others' behaviors. But theories often feel overly abstract or detached from the realities of life for busy librarians. And theories do not always seem practical. So how can the gulf between the abstract and the practical be narrowed so theories can become tools librarians incorporate into their everyday work? Combining aspects of theory with practical, everyday observations and actions is the role of praxis. Working from a praxis framework means seeking out opportunities for reflection on day-to-day experiences so you can better understand what is happening around you and then make changes as a result of those reflections. This book provides one way to reflect on the behaviors you have observed, so you can compare and contrast those observations with theories. Each chapter will walk through reference, instruction, and outreach examples based on the selected theories. This chapter will discuss what theories are and how they can be used, and will introduce a particular set of theories—student development theories—that have been underexplored in librarianship but that can inspire the programs librarians create, as well as influence the way librarians cultivate individual interactions with learners.

A Brief Primer on Using Theories

Most librarians' education included courses that discussed theories relevant to library and information sciences. Depending on what era you were enrolled in library school, you may have studied Marcia Bates's Berrypicking Model (Bates 1989), Carol Kuhlthau's Information Search Process (Kuhlthau 2004), David Kolb's Experiential Learning Theory (Kolb, Boyatzis, and Mainemelis 2001), or Richard Delgado and Jean Stefancic's Critical Race Theory (Delgado and Stefancic 2012). The reason theories are covered in classes on library instruction or information organization, or in an introduction to reference services is typically to establish a shared understanding of how the profession has developed, as well as to provide a better understanding of library users. For graduate students who plan to continue doing academic research throughout their careers, theory will serve as a framework for their research practices. But for librarians who work in public libraries, school libraries, special libraries, and academic libraries, theory can be used to inform their work as practitioners. While graduate school coursework can provide an introduction into how to translate theory into practice, reflecting on how theory relates to your current work context gives a more grounded way for practitioners to learn from theories. Because not all librarians naturally gravitate toward exploring theories or have had the time to practice using theories, this chapter will introduce an overview of what theories are, how they are developed, and how they can be used, so you can develop a framework for incorporating the theories in this book into your practice.

What Are Theories?

Theories are generated in an intentional way by researchers who are following the methods and practices of their discipline. Theories are not simply a pithy phrase based on someone's happenstance speculations. Instead, theories are developed by collecting a lot of information, over a wide variety of situations, and then summarizing that information (see figure 1.1). As researchers distill information into a theory, they look for patterns or an overarching framework that helps to simply explain the behaviors or relationships they have observed. The goal of a theory is to explain trends over a broad range of experiences. Because theories are trying to bring together many ideas into a more easily digestible single idea, they provide general rather than extremely specific descriptions.

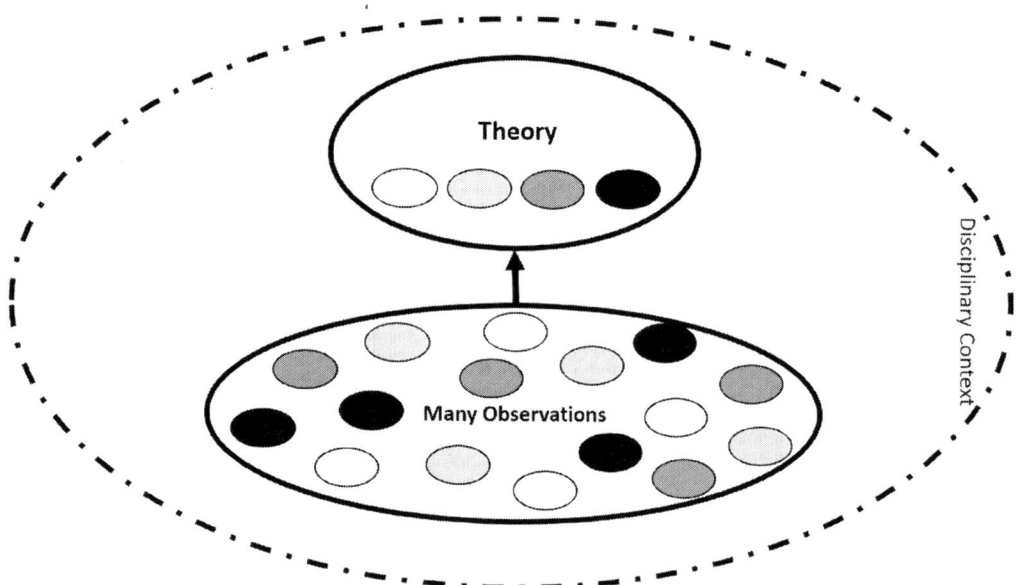

Figure 1.1. How theories are developed

While it can be tempting to conflate theories with common sense, theories have several key defining characteristics that separate them from commonsense observations (Mitchell and Jolley 2007). Good theories are

- consistent with themselves;
- grounded in facts;
- able to make new, surprising predictions;
- capable of organizing, summarizing, and explaining a set of facts; and
- testable.

These characteristics can be contrasted with characteristics of common sense. Observations made solely based on common sense can have the following less desirable qualities:

- They may be contradictory.
- They are not necessarily connected to facts but rely on intuition.

- They are inclined toward making obvious predictions.
- They may oversimplify facts.
- They are not designed to be tested.

Librarians have many day-to-day experiences that can be shaped into a commonsense understanding of the way users interact with the library. These observations are based on expertise that is gained over time and impact the way librarians think about the types of sources learners should use, the way teenage or adult learners interact with the library, how new technologies are promoted, and how instruction sessions are structured. Many of these observations are valuable and help librarians make decisions and choices that positively affect their users. However, when librarians only draw on everyday experiences, without systematically testing those assumptions or checking to see if other librarians in different circumstances are observing similar phenomena, the result can be the oversimplification or misrepresentation of a situation (see examples in table 1.1). In contrast, theories such as the Adult Learning Theory and the Library Anxiety Theory are consistent, grounded in facts, and have been tested in multiple contexts. As a result, those theories can be used by both scholars and practitioners.

In some fields, theories may be intended solely for use by other scholars who will then try to either refute the theory or connect it to their own observations. But theories can also be intended for use by practitioners who apply theories to real-life situations where the effectiveness of the theory can be witnessed in action. If circumstances change and the theory doesn't apply any more, theories are expected to change or else be discarded if they are no longer relevant (Mitchell and Jolley 2007). Theories are not meant to be clung to forever without evidence that the theory is still meaningful—this is especially true for practitioners who may see rapid changes in their user demographics or the technological landscape.

How Are Theories Used?

Theories are often described as having four uses: description, explanation, prediction, and control (Evans et al. 2010). *Description* provides an overview of the behavior; *explanation* describes why the behavior is happening; *prediction* offers the likely outcome to behaviors if certain changes are made to the system; and *control* explores what changes will cause particular behaviors to happen (see figure 1.2). However, not all theories have all of these characteristics.

Theories are used in many disciplines. But each field thinks about and uses theories in a way that matches their context. In some fields, theories are more like laws and predict and model how things will work in a very consistent way. For example, because of what physicists know about the theory of gravity, they can reliably predict how objects on earth will behave as compared to objects on the moon. Germ theory, which was referenced earlier, is used in medicine and influences the way doctors work with all patients and doesn't vary based on a patient's gender or age. As a result, doctors are able to control certain physiological responses in patients. However, in the social sciences, theories describe human behaviors that often vary based on age, gender, socioeconomic status, and many other variables. Humans aren't machines that can be experimented with and expected to behave the same way every time. As a result, social science theories—including education, librarianship, and many information science theories—usually don't try to predict or control how people will behave (Evans et al. 2010). Instead these theories describe behaviors

Table 1.1. Characteristics of theories and common sense with examples from library and information science

CHARACTERISTICS OF THEORIES[1]	LIS THEORY EXAMPLES	CHARACTERISTICS OF COMMON SENSE	LIBRARY EXAMPLES BASED ONLY ON COMMON SENSE
Consistent with itself	*Theory of Information Poverty*: Marginalized groups create norms that lead members to hide information from outsiders to avoid stigma.[2]	Can be contradictory	Peer-reviewed articles are the best source of information, but receiving news through a filter bubble destroys democracy.
Grounded in facts	*Adult Learning Theory*: Adult learners have unique learning needs and face a variety of barriers because of economic, family, and job constraints.[3]	Not necessarily connected to facts but relies on intuition	Noticing that adult library users tend to have a harder time using the computers.
May make new, surprising predictions	*Gartner's Hype Cycle*: New technologies aren't adopted in a positive, linear way, but instead go through an up-and-down cycle before being more slowly adopted.[4]	Makes obvious predictions	Once a few, key people hear about this new service our library is offering, everyone is going to want to use it.
Organizes, summarizes, and explains a set of facts	*Library Anxiety Theory*: Uncomfortable emotions triggered by being in a library setting result in a decreased ability to become information literate.[5]	Can oversimplify facts	First-year students are afraid of going into big buildings such as the library by themselves.
Testable	*Dweck's Theories of Intelligence*: Questions from Dweck's survey were used to determine whether reference and instruction librarians are more likely to view intelligence as something people are born with or that is developed over time.[6]	Not designed to be tested	Assuming first impressions about whether a class will understand how to use databases are almost always right.

Notes

1. Adapted from Mitchell and Jolley 2007.
2. Chatman 1996.
3. Gold 2005.
4. Washburn 2011.
5. Mellon 1986.
6. Folk 2016.

in a logical way so that everyone can work from the same definitions. And social science theories explain behaviors so that practitioners have a greater understanding of why people behave the way they do.

Librarians have used theories to better understand and make decisions about a host of issues facing librarianship including users' information-seeking behaviors, the way that service points within libraries should be designed, how to moderate learners' feelings of library anxiety, best practices for working with underserved populations, and how

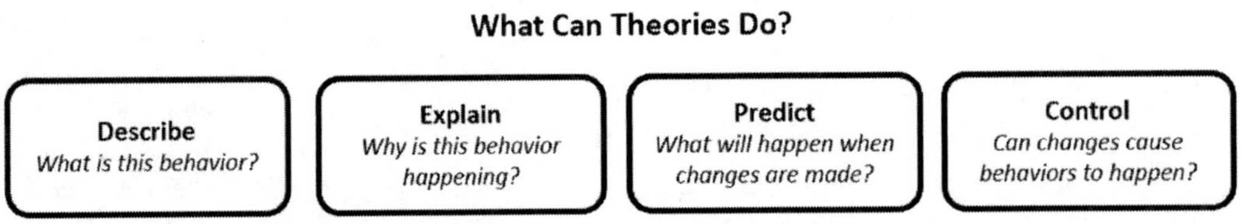

What Can Theories Do?

Describe	Explain	Predict	Control
What is this behavior?	Why is this behavior happening?	What will happen when changes are made?	Can changes cause behaviors to happen?

Figure 1.2. Four possible uses for theory

librarians' perceptions of learners' intelligence impact the way reference and instruction is provided. These theories aren't rules that librarians have to follow but instead provide helpful frameworks for approaching big problems in new ways. Several examples of theories frequently referenced in librarianship are included in the box below.

EXAMPLES OF THEORIES USED IN LIBRARY AND INFORMATION SCIENCE

Zipf's Principle of Least Effort. Zipf's theory states that people complete tasks by choosing the path that involves the least effort (Zipf 1949, as cited in Chang 2016). Librarians have used this theory to explain how searchers use databases and other search tools.

Dweck's Theories of Intelligence. Dweck's theories of intelligence include two opposing theories. Entity theory describes level of intelligence as fixed, something people are born with. Incremental theory describes intelligence as developing over time based on interactions with the world (Dweck 1999, as cited in Folk 2016). Librarians have used this theory to explain how reference and instruction librarians think about their learners and the impacts of subscribing to either entity or incremental theory.

Library Anxiety Theory. Library anxiety explains students' fear of the library space and using library sources (Mellon 1986). Librarians have used this theory to provide more targeted activities to familiarize incoming students with library spaces, to create more welcoming spaces, and to educate academic instructors about students' fear of using the library.

Why Do Theories Matter?

Librarians have mixed feelings about theories or guiding frameworks. Examples of some librarians' ambivalence toward using theories can be observed in the conversations that took place around the adoption of the 2016 Association of College and Research Libraries (ACRL) Framework for Information Literacy for Higher Education. Some librarians felt that the framework was elitist and did not give enough practical, easily implementable solutions (Bombaro 2016). But others felt that the use of a broad theory provided flexibility for librarians who work in diverse environments (Farkas 2016). This tension has existed in social science disciplines for many years (see the box on page 7 for examples from psychology and education) and reflects a common divide between researchers and practitioners. Because this book is written for practitioners, the discussion will focus on why theories should matter to practicing librarians.

EXAMPLES OF THE DIVIDE BETWEEN RESEARCHERS AND PRACTITIONERS

Many psychologists working today in an applied field are keenly aware of the need for close cooperation between theoretical and applied psychology. This can be accomplished in psychology, as it has been accomplished in physics, if the theorist does not look toward applied problems with highbrow aversion or with a fear of social problems, and if the applied psychologist realizes that there is nothing so practical as a good theory.
—Kurt Lewin, prominent social psychology researcher (1951, 169)

Some if not many of the pre-service and in-service teachers in my courses, however, are nearly singular in pursuit of the practical. Anything theoretical is impractical, anything from the past is outdated—if not directly spoken, these are often the attitudes of these [K–12 English teacher] practitioners.
—P. L. Thomas, professor of education and former high school English teacher (2011)

Describing a complex or underrecognized issue is one of the most important functions of a theory. Theories can also provide clear definitions of concepts. For example, Paula Beer (2012), an information communication technology teacher in the UK who worked with elementary school students, wanted to apply Jerome Bruner's theories on discovery learning and play to her work environment. Play may seem like a simple concept, but not all people in all cultural situations think of play in the same way. Because the theory of play describes the idea of "play" in a specific way, others can use Bruner's theory and apply it in their own context based on this particular understanding of play. However, not all theories are well defined. For example, student development theories are noted for their lack of clear definitions (Evans et al. 2010). Sometimes theories are left intentionally vague to enhance their flexibility across more situations. But in other cases, the theorists may have ignored the defining role of theories in order to focus on explanation or other functions of theories.

Theories also matter because they get at experiences and observations that are not easy to understand. In some fields, this may be because the phenomenon explored is too small, perhaps the concepts are too abstract, or the organisms or people observed are too different. Alternatively, the behavior explored may be something that is so commonplace, such as individual thoughts or feelings, that few people stop to take an in-depth look at the behavior. By pulling these hard-to-understand or underobserved questions together into a theory, the issues become easier to understand, and it is possible to come up with solutions or strategies for the problems raised by the theory.

Finally, theories provide an understanding of the history of a field based not just on anecdotes but on recorded, research-based perspectives. Because theories are distributed in the scholarly literature, there is a record of them that can be examined over time to see how a field has changed, what theories have been adopted for a time and then discarded, and what a particular profession values at any point in time. For example, an exploration of the way librarians and information scientists have understood knowledge over time might reveal a shift from a more centralized, top-down approach to knowledge creation, to a more populist, user-centered approach to knowledge creation. This shift could be observed in the design of search tools and in the way learners are encouraged to use their libraries' physical and virtual spaces.

Transitioning to the Practical

Theories are used to describe, explain, and sometimes predict and control behaviors. But how do those principles translate into actually using theories in regular work practice? Two, somewhat overlapping, approaches will be discussed here. The first approach is to use theories as an individual guide. The second approach is to use theories as a place for starting discussions with groups.

Individual Practice

Educational psychologist Jerome Bruner (2006) described theories as a guide to get you from where you are to where you want to be. Theories can spark your thinking and help generate ideas that you may not have otherwise considered. Those sparks can then act as a guide for goal-setting activities for yourself or your library. For example, after reading about the theory of library anxiety, a public services librarian may be more inclined to reflect on how users of their library display signs of anxiety. Based on these observations, this librarian could set a goal related to instruction and outreach or tied to how the physical space is designed (see table 1.2).

Continued observation, reflection, and discussion are key elements of praxis, which brings together theory and practice. Reflection comes more naturally to some people than others, and learning new reflective behaviors takes repeated practice. The following section discusses three options for expanding the ways you can reflect on the observations you make as a librarian.

Journaling is a reflective activity that many people find to be beneficial. Journaling is frequently used to record personal, non-work-related thoughts and feelings, but journal-

Table 1.2. Example of using theory as a guide for setting goals

THEORY	LOCAL REFLECTIONS	GOALS
Library Anxiety Theory: Uncomfortable emotions triggered by being in a library setting result in a decreased ability to become information literate.[1]	• International students seem hesitant to check out books.	• Create contacts in the international student office, and explore the possibility of offering a welcome to the library session for international students.
	• Few undergraduate students approach the reference desk, which is an enormous oak structure, located on the second floor of the library.	• Draft proposal to try out smaller reference desk stations closer to the entry on the main floor of the library.

Note

1. Mellon 1986.

ing can also be used to record ideas after work events such as an outreach activity or an instruction session. Recording observations over time provides a longitudinal record and can reveal that larger trends are emerging in the work you do. Journaling can also show where small changes have occurred. For example, journaling about an instruction session that you found to be difficult can generate ideas for making changes the next time you teach it. Journaling after making those changes helps maintain a record of what works and doesn't work and can alleviate the stress that comes from facing a situation that triggers negative emotions. Looking back on a record of those changes can help you see how your practice is evolving and what has shaped those changes.

Another individual reflective practice is close listening. Some beginning techniques for slowing down and reflecting by listening include making time for short periods of silent listening and listening to everyday sounds such as those you might encounter in your library's coffee shop or in a busy entryway (Treasure 2011). Listening closely can help you to focus your thoughts but can also help you become more aware of what is happening around you. Working at the reference desk provides many opportunities for listening. Not only is there an opportunity to listen to learners' direct questions, but also listening to the general hum and flow of conversations taking place around the desk may reveal struggles learners are having or concerns that are unique to particular times of the term. Reflecting on what you have heard can lead to a higher degree of empathy and a greater understanding of your learners' needs.

One more way to shape a reflective practice is through reading. Librarians are obvious proponents of reading, but it may be difficult to carve out time for reflective reading. However, setting aside time to read reflectively is a key way to develop new understanding. Reading provides a window into others' experiences and can be especially beneficial if you select a range of viewpoints to read that are different from your own. Many genres are able to provide a diverse reading experience. Journal articles and book chapters give insights into libraries and projects that may be different from the environment at your library. Fiction can allow you to imagine what life was like for someone in another time period or place. Following a wide range of people on social media gives you the opportunity to see how people of different races, ethnicities, sexual orientations, or nation of origin currently think about issues and respond to events. Reading reflectively doesn't mean you need to submit a research report after reading each scholarly article or that you need to agree with everything you read on Twitter. But through comparing and contrasting what you read with your own experience, a more informed understanding of others' behaviors can emerge. See table 1.3 for examples of using reflective practices in reference, instruction, and outreach.

INDIVIDUAL REFLECTIVE PRACTICES

- Journaling
- Close listening
- Reading broadly

Table 1.3. Examples of individual reflective practices used in reference, instruction, and outreach settings and the observations made by using these practices

	REFLECTIVE PRACTICE	OBSERVATIONS
Reference	Close listening at the reference desk	• Students are frustrated with the inability to find open computers for quick printing at the middle and end of each term. • At the beginning and ends of the term, students are looking for fiction to read and other ways to relieve stress.
Instruction	Reading several library instruction blogs	• Even though student demographics are different, search behaviors seem to be consistent with what librarians at other schools are observing. • Instruction librarians at other institutions don't rely on standards in the same way that librarians at your institution do.
Outreach	Journaling after annual new student orientation events	• Fewer incoming first-year students are familiar with what librarians do. • Students increasingly refer to their phones during orientation activities.

Group Practice

Adult and continuing education professor Jack Mezirow (2000) argued that praxis comes about because of the interaction between understanding theory and taking action. This interaction often takes place in the form of discussions with colleagues who push each other to develop deeper understandings about why certain things are happening in their library. Because theory provides common language and a general summary of many observations, theory can also be used to bring together larger communities of practice that share interests and concerns. While communities of practice include people with many similar values and experiences, not all members will work in the exact same types of institutions or serve the same types of learners. As a result, theories can provide a starting point for discussions between community members who have different frames of reference. The #critlib community (http://critlib.org/) is an example of an online community that brings together librarians from public, academic, and special libraries to discuss their various experiences and approaches to critical librarianship. The ideas of critical librarianship are grounded in theories such as critical pedagogy, critical race theory, and critical reflection.

Creating spaces for reflection in groups is also an important component of moving from theory to practice. As librarian Kevin Seeber (2016) notes, collective reflection is often an avenue to new insights. While reflection in groups has some similarities with individual reflective approaches, not all the approaches are identical. Reflection through writing can also be used in groups. Scheduling time for journaling a response to a question or issue in meetings is a technique that can be used to allow time for participants to think more deeply or to give people who are more reticent to speak time to gather their thoughts. Blogging is another way that reflections can be shared with a larger group outside of your immediate geographic sphere.

Listening is a reflective practice that groups can exercise as well. However, within group settings, the emphasis shifts toward open listening and asking intentional questions. Question asking is a vital part of listening in groups. Asking questions that are open-ended and show respect for others by listening intently creates an environment of respectful engagement where diverse voices are heard and new ideas are more likely to emerge (Carmeli, Dutton, and Hardin 2015). In addition, asking questions driven by curiosity about what other group members know or have experienced can open up new possibilities for the group to explore. Dawna Markova and Angie McArthur (2015) refer to the higher levels of intellectual diversity that result from good listening and question asking as collaborative intelligence. Developing collaborative intelligence involves a commitment from group members to listen to ideas that may be unfamiliar or uncomfortable but can result in more creative and productive working environments.

Reading is usually a solitary activity, but reflecting on new insights gained from exploring new scholarly literature, reading a new blog post, or scanning through a new Twitter feed with a group of fellow practitioners can be a fruitful way to multiply the insights gained. Consider reserving some time on a monthly basis in a departmental meeting to discuss new ideas based on what the group has been reading. Alternatively, start a journal club, book club, or Twitter club with people in your library who have a range of responsibilities, or with colleagues from a neighboring library. Some groups may choose to read the same thing, while other groups may prefer to share based on the range of readings they have encountered in the past month. Jointly reflecting on what has been read and listening to other perspectives can enhance practice in unexpected ways.

GROUP REFLECTIVE PRACTICES

- Reflective writing in meetings or blogging
- Open listening and question asking
- Discussing readings in a group

Theories can also be used in groups to develop shared benchmarks or assessment tools that practitioners from various institutions can then use to create a shared discussion around the assessment of their work. For example, many academic instruction librarians agree with ideas promoted by constructivist theory and create similar learning outcomes based on this joint starting premise. As a result, instruction assessment tools such as rubrics can be shared across institutions, and results from multiple institutions can be pooled to gain a greater understanding of what learners know about information literacy. For another example of using theories to start shared discussions, see the box below.

> **THEORY AS A FACILITATOR FOR SHARED DISCUSSION EXAMPLE**
>
> A presentation on library anxiety was given at a regional consortial library meeting. In addition to explaining library anxiety theory and several of the ways that the theory has been applied, the speaker noted specific user groups that were more prone to experiencing library anxiety and provided ideas for making libraries more welcoming and friendly. During the lunch break that followed, librarians from a range of community colleges, private colleges, and large state universities sat together and discussed how they had all observed instances of library anxiety in their international student populations. Some of the schools only served undergraduate international students and others had both undergraduate and graduate international students, but each of the librarians noticed similar patterns in the anxieties displayed by their students. They agreed that contacting their respective international student offices to advocate for targeted library instruction for international students would be a good first step. Then one of the librarians mentioned that she had just received a grant to develop an online tutorial. She suggested that she could focus the tutorial on needs specific to international students. She offered to share the resulting tutorial with all of the consortium members, who could then distribute it to their international programs offices. All of the lunch partners thought this sounded like a great idea. They agreed to try out the tutorial at their own schools, assess how well the tutorial worked for their students, and to check in after one school year had passed.
>
> When these librarians reconvened at the following year's regional meeting, they discussed the shared successes and failures of the tutorial approach. Some of the librarians observed that their students were too different from the students at other schools because of cultural variations resulting from their country of origin and had decided to use other approaches to alleviate their students' library anxiety. However, after suggesting some tweaks to the tutorial, other librarians felt they would like to continue using the shared tool to combat library anxiety at their institution.

Finally, theories can be helpful tools for explaining the work librarians do to stakeholders outside of the library such as social services personnel, academic faculty, or technology workers. Many of the theories used by librarians draw on the fields of psychology, sociology, education, communication, and technology, and as a result can serve as a bridge to establishing connections with people who have overlapping interests in those fields. Backing up proposals with theories is also a powerful way to demonstrate to administrators or funding agencies that the work of librarians is grounded in a thoughtful, systematic approach.

Cautions on Using Theory

There are a few cautions to be mindful of as you begin integrating theory into your practice. Theories are not intended to box you in or to create artificial rules or boundaries. When describing a particular theory, it can often appear that only one theory is being used at a time. However, because most librarians have different responsibilities and interactions with a range of learners, theories are typically used in combination, or a variety of theories are used for different projects. Using multiple theories is called an integrative approach and recognizes that people and workplace settings are complex and that the expertise of the practitioner is needed to make sound decisions based on local needs (Evans et al. 2010).

Using theory in practice should always be grounded and adapted to your local needs and your knowledge of your community. Because theories are more general, you will need to consider what elements actually apply to your local context. Your learners and users are real people and as a result their actions can't be easily predicted or controlled. Your user population will also be unique in some ways. Perhaps you are on a commuter campus, you work at an elementary school that serves many developmentally challenged students, or your institution may recruit from a particular geographic region. Each of these populations may behave in ways that are different from the specific learners upon whom a particular theory was based. Several ideas for learning more about your learner population will be discussed toward the end of the chapter.

Introduction to Student Development Theories

The remainder of this book will focus on a set of theories known as student development theories. A brief overview of the historical background of student development theories and how they are used is discussed next. In addition, a rationale for why student development theories are important for the work librarians do is provided along with some ways to start building a better understanding of your local context so these theories can be incorporated in an appropriate and strategic way.

Student development theories were first generated in the middle of the last century based on observations and research done on college campuses. As opposed to learning theories, which tend to emphasize what takes place in more traditional learning settings such as classrooms, student development theories grew out of the work of student affairs offices and therefore focused on learning that takes place in less-structured learning environments such as student clubs, residence halls, and via service opportunities. Student development theories are interested in many different factors that impact students so that programs and services can be created that acknowledge students' behaviors in a more holistic way. As a result, there is not a single, comprehensive student development theory but instead many student development theories that cover issues such as how students' thinking and reasoning (or intellect) develops over time, how students' sense of self or identity changes, and how students choose to engage in activities outside of the classroom. These theories are informed by the many external factors influencing students' lives (see figure 1.3). Student affairs professionals work in a range of settings and groups including residence halls, Greek life housing, and off-campus student groups, and in roles such as counselors and advisors (Evans et al. 2010).

Many similarities can be found between the work student affairs professionals do and the work librarians do. Both groups facilitate experiences and spaces that enhance student learning, often while working outside of a more traditional, graded classroom setting. Academic librarians may interact more with traditional college-age students than other types of librarians, but all librarians share the vision of creating lifelong learners. Consequently, librarians are also interested in a holistic view of students and seek to understand what students' information-seeking needs are beyond their college years. Librarian Julie

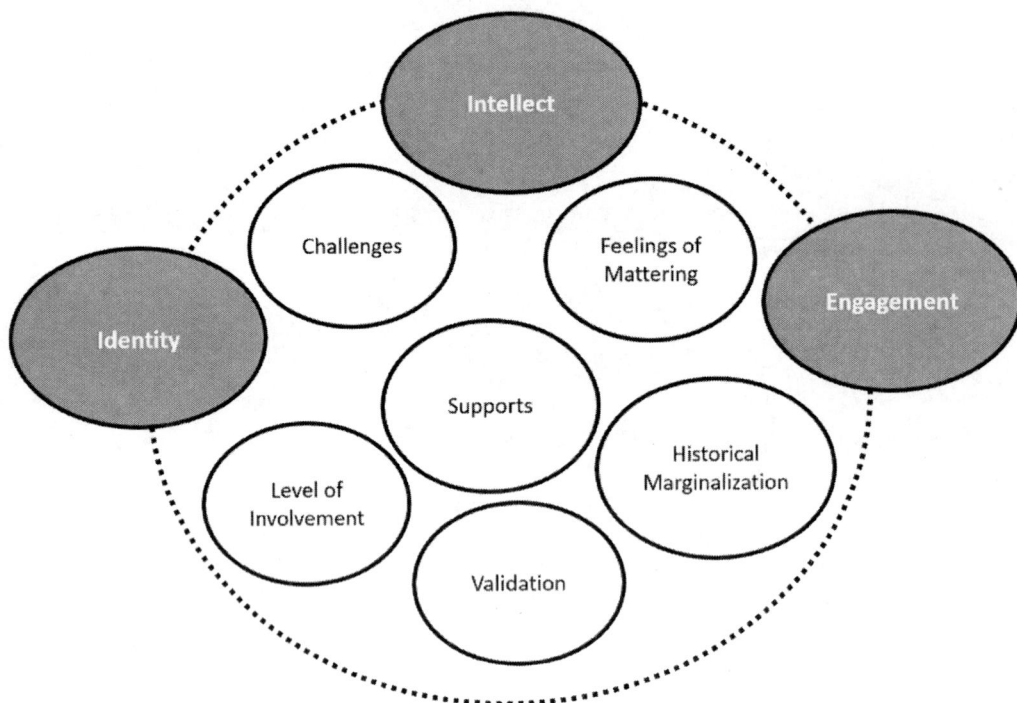

Figure 1.3. Student development theories and influencing factors

Mitchell and accessibility advisor Margot Bell (2012) note that incorporating student development theories into the library environment demonstrates a larger shift toward placing students at the center of libraries' work. Understanding differences in how people approach information due to their developmental stage can help librarians to be more proactive, understanding, and intentional in the way reference, instruction, and outreach services are provided to all learners.

This book will focus on three main student development theory groups: intellectual development theories, identity theory, and engagement theory. These theories were chosen because of their long-standing importance and use in the student affairs field, as well as because of their relevance to libraries. Before beginning to explore these theories, it is important to examine your own context and to find out as much as possible about your own learner population prior to making decisions or judgments based on these theories. Data to help inform the way you incorporate theory into practice can be gathered at both an institutional and at a more granular level.

Institutional data to explore include surveys that examine students' attitudes toward campus services, study habits, perceptions of educational opportunities, and students' overall sense of the campus climate. Several nationwide surveys are used at many institutions to collect this data. Some examples include the NSSE, the National Survey of Student Engagement, and the BCSSE, Beginning College Survey of Student Engagement. In addition, many campuses conduct their own campus climate surveys. Institutions also collect information about student demographics that can help you get a better picture of the range of ages, races, and ethnicities represented on your campus. Begin by checking the "About" section on your institution's website, reports on the president's website, or with your registrar's office. You may also be able to learn how many students transfer from other institutions, receive need-based aid, or are the first in their families to attend college. All of these components of students' lives demonstrate what kind of variability in past experiences your students have and will influence the way they experience the services they encounter on campus.

Alternatively, if you do not work in an academic setting, consider seeking out information from city climate surveys. Explore demographic reports for your local area, and look for changes in population that may be happening over time. City, county, and state websites can all be sources of information about your local population, especially if they break down census information for your area. School district websites may be another valuable source of information about your learner population, including such information as the number of students who receive free lunches or the languages spoken by your learner population.

More specific and nuanced information can be gathered from smaller groups of learners such as those in a class or workshop. To avoid making unfounded assumptions about learners, consider asking a few relevant questions at the beginning of a session to frame your understanding of their experiences. In a library instruction session, you could ask questions about students' technology use, for example, what devices do they typically use to search for information; how comfortable are they with troubleshooting technological problems; and who do they ask for help with technological or information-based needs. A workshop introducing primary source documents from the archives could begin with questions that help you understand students' generational differences. For example, you could ask what students perceive as the defining moments for their generation, or where they think their generation seeks out information. These questions could both inform your understanding of these students' past experiences, especially if the class is composed of a diverse range of ages, and could be used to compare and contrast with the historical documents explored in the session. Instead of assuming you already know what your students are thinking or feeling ahead of time, find out from the students themselves.

Finally, one additional component that informs how you think about theories and how they are applied is you. Your background, including educational experiences, family dynamics, gender, ethnicity, and other shaping factors, all influence how you conceptualize the behaviors you observe. Reflect on these influences by asking how and when do my background experiences and identities lead me to make assumptions about how others will process information or think about their own identity? Thinking critically about your own assumptions can help you to be open to the different experiences and influences your learners bring.

Key Points

Understanding how theories are generated, how they are intended to be used, and what contextual cues to look for to make theories relevant for your work situation help create programs and services based in a broader understanding of others' behaviors and experiences. Here are some key points to take away:

- Theories are generated using the guidelines and expectations of a particular disciplinary area, and each discipline creates and uses theories somewhat differently.
- Social science theories can be used to describe and explain behaviors in simple, but sometimes surprising ways.
- Using reflection and data about your unique learner population helps incorporate theories into your local library practice.

- Student development theories focus on learning experiences outside of traditional classroom settings and consider many factors impacting students' lives.

Chapter 2 will guide you through a foundational student development theory that explores how students develop intellectually and offers examples of library programs that can enhance students learning at different stages of intellectual growth.

References

ACRL (Association of College and Research Libraries). 2016. "Framework for Information Literacy for Higher Education." January 11. http://www.ala.org/.

Bates, Marcia J. 1989. "The Design of Browsing and Berrypicking Techniques for the Online Search Interface." *Online Review* 13 (5): 407–24.

Beer, Paula. 2012. "The Process of Technology Learning: Applying Bruner's Theory on Play, Discovery and Cultural Learning to the Acquisition of ICT Capability." In *Applying Theory to Educational Research: An Introductory Approach with Case Studies*, edited by Jeff Adams, Matt Cochrane, and Linda Dunne, 61–74. Hoboken, NJ: Wiley.

Bombaro, Christine. 2016. "The Framework Is Elitist." *Reference Services Review* 44 (4): 552–63.

Bruner, Jerome S. 2006. *In Search of Pedagogy: The Selected Works of Jerome Bruner, 1957–1978*. New York: Routledge.

Carmeli, Abraham, Jane E. Dutton, and Ashley E. Hardin. 2015. "Respect as an Engine for New Ideas: Linking Respectful Engagement, Relational Information Processing and Creativity among Employees and Teams." *Human Relations* 68 (6): 1021–47. doi:10.1177/0018726714550256.

Chang, Yu-Wei. 2016. "Influence of Human Behavior and the Principle of Least Effort on Library and Information Science Research." *Information Processing and Management* 52 (4): 658–69. doi:10.1016/j.ipm.2015.12.011.

Chatman, Elfreda A. 1996. "The Impoverished Life-World of Outsiders." *Journal of the American Society for Information Science* 47 (3): 193–206.

Delgado, Richard, and Jean Stefancic. 2012. *Critical Race Theory*. New York: NYU Press.

Evans, Nancy J., Deanna S. Forney, Florence M. Guido, Lori D. Patton, and Kristen A. Renn. 2010. *Student Development in College: Theory, Research, and Practice*. 2nd ed. Jossey-Bass Higher and Adult Education Series. San Francisco: Jossey-Bass.

Farkas, Meredith Gorran. 2016. "Is the Framework Elitist? Is ACRL?" Information Wants to Be Free. October 18. http://meredith.wolfwater.com/.

Folk, Amanda L. 2016. "Academic Reference and Instruction Librarians and Dweck's Theories of Intelligence." *College and Research Libraries* 77 (3): 302–13. doi:10.5860/crl.77.3.302.

Gold, Helen E. 2005. "Engaging the Adult Learner: Creating Effective Library Instruction." *portal: Libraries and the Academy* 5 (4): 467–81. doi:10.1353/pla.2005.0051.

Kolb, David A., Richard E. Boyatzis, and Charalampos Mainemelis. 2001. "Experiential Learning Theory: Previous Research and New Directions." In *Perspectives on Thinking, Learning, and Cognitive Styles*, edited by R. J. Sternberg and Li-fang Zhang, 227–47. Educational Psychology Series. Mahwah, NJ: Lawrence Erlbaum Associates.

Kuhlthau, Carol Collier. 2004. *Seeking Meaning: A Process Approach to Library and Information Services*. 2nd ed. Westport, CT: Libraries Unlimited.

Lewin, Kurt. 1951. *Field Theory in Social Science: Selected Theoretical Papers*. 1st ed. New York: Harper & Brothers.

Markova, Dawna, and Angie McArthur. 2015. *Collaborative Intelligence: Thinking with People Who Think Differently*. New York: Spiegel & Grau.

Mellon, Constance A. 1986. "Library Anxiety: A Grounded Theory and Its Development." *College and Research Libraries* 47 (2): 160–65.

Mezirow, Jack. 2000. *Learning as Transformation: Critical Perspectives on a Theory in Progress*. 1st ed. Jossey-Bass Higher and Adult Education Series. San Francisco: Jossey-Bass.

Mitchell, Julie, and Margot Bell. 2012. "Common Ground: UBC Library and Student Development in the Chapman Learning Commons." In *Environments for Student Growth and Development: Libraries and Student Affairs in Collaboration*, edited by Lisa Janicke Hinchliffe, and Melissa Autumn Wong, 151–64. Chicago: Association of College and Research Libraries.

Mitchell, Mark L., and Janina M. Jolley. 2007. "Advantages of Using Theory to Generate Ideas." Research Design Explained. http://www.jolley-mitchell.com/.

Seeber, Kevin. 2016. "Who Benefits?" *Kevin Seeper/MLIS* (blog), December 19. http://kevinseeber.com/blog/who-benefits.

Thomas, P. L. 2011. "A Respect for the Past, a Knowledge of the Present, and a Concern for the Future': The Role of History in English Education." *English Education* 43 (2): 123–44.

Treasure, Julian. 2011. "5 Ways to Listen Better." TED Talk. https://www.ted.com/.

Washburn, Bruce. 2011. "Library Mobile Applications: What Counts as Success?" *Information Outlook* 15 (1): 13–16.

CHAPTER 2

Encouraging Intellectual Growth

IN THIS CHAPTER

▷ Understanding how learners develop the ability to make meaning from a wide variety of information sources

▷ Interpreting how learners' intellectual development influences the way they think about authority and evidence

▷ Creating a safe environment for reference interactions that support intellectual development

▷ Designing instruction sessions appropriate for learners' intellectual development phases

▷ Planning outreach activities that shift learners' view of authority and evidence

HAVE YOU EVER HAD A STUDENT come to the reference desk asking for help finding scholarly articles, only to realize the student has no clear understanding of what these articles are or why the instructor was asking for them? Have you ever observed students selecting the top two or three results in a search results list with no consideration for the quality or authority of those sources? Or have you ever had a student in a reference consultation ask you for advice about how to work with their advisors or major professors?

At the heart of each of those questions is an interpretation about how learners make meaning from different types of evidence and perceive authority in a variety of new contexts. Librarians constantly deal with issues related to authority and meaning-making in their work. Depending on what kind of library work you do, the idea of authority may be understood in a variety of ways. For example, catalogers are highly familiar with the concept of authority control. Much of their work involves standardizing the way information is presented so that searchers can consistently and predictably find information.

Because of their expertise, catalogers can provide authority for information that was previously unordered. Instruction librarians may think about authority in a somewhat different way. For example, the ACRL Information Literacy Framework emphasizes the importance of recognizing how authority is viewed depending on different contexts in the frame "authority is constructed and contextual" (ACRL 2016). In practice, instruction librarians often use this concept to teach students to examine the differences between peer-reviewed and popular literature. One distinguishing factor often emphasized about these two source types is that the editing process used and the authors' expertise signal how much authority the source has. Instruction librarians work to make those distinctions clear so that students are able to classify similar sources in new contexts, while recognizing that the line between source types can be fuzzy and that there isn't always an absolute right answer.

Depending on your past library experiences, you may have experienced authority in both of those contexts, as well as in many other aspects of your personal and professional life. However, once you learned how to make meaning in a new context, you likely stopped thinking explicitly about how those connections were made. For example, with repeated experience, evaluating the difference between a peer-reviewed and a popular article is a process your brain can handle in a few seconds. Your mind automatically sorts out how authority was determined for the different types of information. Moreover, if you encounter a slightly different format of the scholarly article, for example, an HTML version of the article rather than a printed article in a bound journal, you would be able to transfer your preexisting understanding about scholarly articles so that you could still determine the authority of the article despite the difference in format. Or if you were asked to choose the best source for presenting to a specific audience, you would likely be able to adjust and understand that a less scholarly source may be more appropriate. But for novices these activities can be hurdles that require significant thought before the learner can determine how to best use the information presented.

The ability to understand where authority comes from, when to rely on intuition, and when to adapt your sense of authority to a new situation are all intellectual processes that start to happen reflexively. However, an understanding of authority and how to make meaning when confronted with increasingly complex questions doesn't just happen automatically at birth. For most people, this changes over time. This chapter will discuss a theory that describes how people's understanding of meaning-making from different sources of evidence and authority change as their experiences impact how they think. This chapter will also discuss how librarians can use this theory to create a broad range of learning experiences.

Cognitive-Structural Theories

The area of student development theory that examines how students think, reason, and make meaning from a diverse array of information, especially as the questions become more complicated, is called Cognitive-Structural Theory. There are several types of cognitive-structural theories. Some focus on moral or faith development, and others focus on intellectual development. All of these theories have different stages that learners progress through at different rates (Long 2012). Most of these theories describe developmental characteristics of upper high school and traditional college-aged students; therefore, the examples in this chapter will primarily focus on that same learner group. However, note that cognitive-structural development continues throughout the life-span and that different people develop at different rates. This chapter will focus on one of the first and most well known intellectual development theories. Chapters 3 and 4 will continue with a focus on several more recent intellectual development theories.

For librarians who teach information literacy concepts, work with students on reference questions, or plan outreach events, developing learners' ability to think, reason, and make meaning in order to find and use information is a regular part of daily practice. Yet because few librarians have received training in student development theories, you may not have a name for the gaps you see in learners' information skills, and as a result it can be easy to either blame your teaching ability or the students' ability to learn when problems arise. Recognizing that the developmental stage at which learners are located impacts the way they make meaning from evidence and understand authority can help shift the approaches used in reference consultations, in the classroom, and in outreach activities to better align with students' stages and promote intellectual growth.

The History of Perry's Intellectual and Ethical Development Theory

One of the most prominent cognitive-structural theories is William Perry's Intellectual and Ethical Development Theory. This theory has spurred other researchers to develop a variety of theories about how students develop their understanding of the world, particularly as they encounter information in conflict with ideas they previously held. Because of the importance of Perry's theory in the field of student development theories, the rest of this chapter will focus on the key principles of this theory, particularly as they relate to the library environment.

As with many student development theories, Perry's Intellectual and Ethical Development Theory grew out of his direct interactions with students. While working at Harvard University as a counselor in the 1950s and 1960s, Perry and several colleagues performed a longitudinal study with male students at Harvard and a few female students at Radcliffe. He and his colleagues interviewed these students at the end of each year for four years and asked them broad, open-ended questions about their experiences over the course of the past year (Perry 1970). Perry tried to interview a diverse range of students. At a predominantly male, almost entirely white institution as was Harvard at the time, diversity in this context meant his sample was made up of students who demonstrated different ways of reacting to intellectual challenges with a range of possible solutions. At first, Perry thought these differences were based on personality traits. But after analyzing the transcripts of the student interviews, Perry and his colleagues began to see patterns in students' responses that indicated the differences were actually related to developmental stages rather than personality.

Perry's theory posits that when faced with new information, a student will take in that information and make meaning from it in different ways depending on the student's intellectual and ethical development stage. Perry and his colleagues came up with a nine-position theory to walk through all of these stages of intellectual and ethical development. The initial positions primarily focused on intellectual development, and only the last few positions discussed ethical development.

One important feature of Perry's theory that distinguishes it from other cognitive-structural theories is the emphasis on how individuals interpret where authority comes from. Perry (1970) defined authority in two ways. Authority (with a capital *A*) indicates a sense of Authority as a source of absolute, right answers; the second definition of authority (with a lowercase *a*) focuses on a more relative source of authority achieved through social interactions. Both types of authority play a role in the three phases of intellectual development. Ways that librarians can help learners understand authority (with a lowercase *a*) will be emphasized throughout the rest of this chapter.

This discussion of Perry's theory will simplify Perry's model and collapse those nine positions down to three phases that focus solely on intellectual development. This modification will make the theory easier to understand and then translate to the library context.

Three Phases of Intellectual Development

The three combined phases of the Intellectual and Ethical Development Theory are *dualism*, *multiplicity*, and *relativism* (see the box below). Learners in the dualism phase believe that right answers exist for everything, and there are specific authorities who have those right answers (Evans et al. 2010; Perry 1970; Perry 1997). While in the dualism phase, learners focus on what *they*—the person in authority, such as the teacher—want; students then work to try to give the teacher exactly that type of content or performance (Perry 1997, 60). The dualism phase usually starts in childhood and can extend through early college (see figure 2.1).

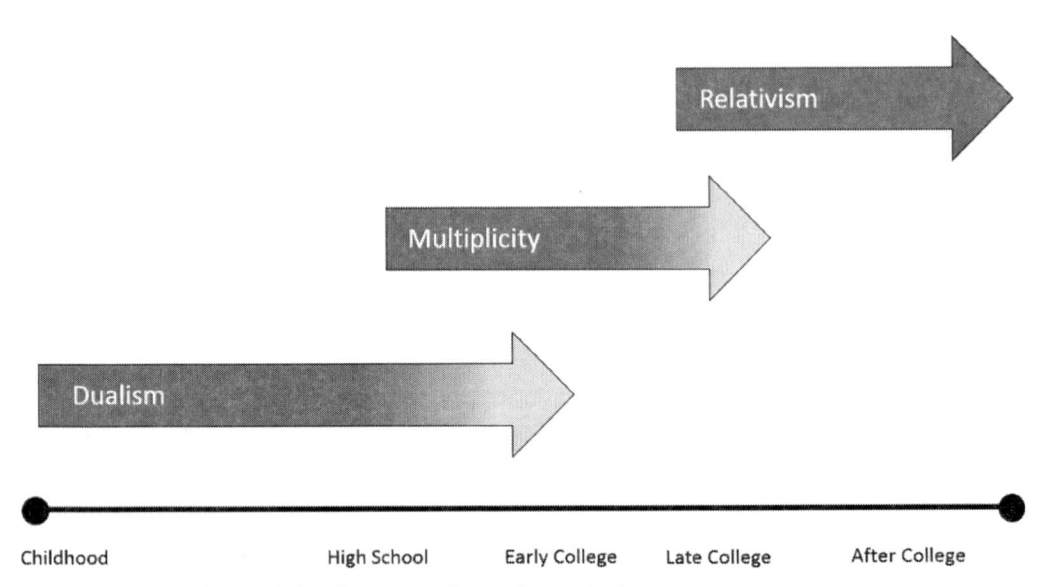

Figure 2.1. Intellectual development phases by typical age range

INTELLECTUAL DEVELOPMENT PHASES

- **Dualism.** Sees the world as black and white; right answers exist for everything, and authorities possess those right answers.
- **Multiplicity.** There are many answers, and anyone can be an authority, one's self included; everyone is entitled to their own opinion; all opinions, including their own, count equally.
- **Relativism.** Not all opinions are equal; context must be considered to make decisions and determine where authority comes from.

Learners in the multiplicity phase begin to think more independently. During the multiplicity phase, learners do a nearly 180 degree turn from the dualism phase and see authority as coming from almost everywhere. Not only do they begin to value themselves as a potential authority with important opinions and viewpoints to share, but also they think everyone else's viewpoint is equally valid. As a result, peers become increasingly valuable sources of information (Evans et al. 2010). When thinking through school assignments, students in the multiplicity phase shift to recognizing there is a particular way the person in authority, that is, the teacher, wants students to do the assignment. Students realize there are specific ways of communicating content that are important to follow and that it's not enough just to present the right content (Perry 1997). The multiplicity phase can start in high school and can last through the later years of college (Perry 1997).

Students who reach the relativism phase believe context needs to be considered when interpreting knowledge. They feel that not all opinions are created equal, and therefore, equal weight shouldn't be given to all ideas, especially to those ideas that aren't well supported. Evidence is required to convince students in the relativism phase that a particular idea or individual should be given authority (Evans et al. 2010). The relativism phase can begin in late college but often doesn't begin until after students have finished college (Perry 1997). See the Information Ethics Workshop Scenario for a real-life example where a librarian grapples with how to work with students at one of these intellectual development phases.

INFORMATION ETHICS WORKSHOP SCENARIO

To better understand these intellectual development phases in a real-world context, picture yourself as the librarian in the following scenario. Ask yourself what intellectual development stage the students are in and how that phase may impact their behaviors.

You are teaching a three-session workshop series on information ethics to first and second-year honors college students as part of their Introduction to Research series. For the first session, you plan a variety of active learning techniques to engage students. However, you notice that while most students listen fairly attentively during the lecture component of your presentation, several of the students don't seem willing to participate in activities with their classmates. When they were asked to compare past experiences with their neighbors, some of these students are obviously checking their phones and are not listening to their peers. At the end of the session, the only questions asked are about the mechanics of the assignment due next week. After the first session, you talk to the course instructor and find out she has also observed that some of the students have trouble in other honors classes when asked to partner with students from different majors. These students have indicated they don't see how working with a fellow student with no expertise in their major is worth their time.

While there may be multiple issues going on with the students in this scenario, the students are displaying several signs of dualistic thinking. First, they see authority as coming from the person in charge of the workshop, and they don't value input from their peers. They feel their classmates' input isn't as valuable as the input from the main authority figure. Second, their focus on the assignment mechanics indicates they are interested in getting the answers right and aren't interested in learning what they feel is extraneous information.

Transitioning between Phases

While the phases in the Intellectual Development theory can reveal interesting issues about students' behavior, what Perry was really interested in were the transition points (Perry 1997). The transition points between phases are where growth can happen and where students may be open to new ways of thinking (see figure 2.2). Instructors and librarians can help foster growth at these transition phases. One of the primary ways educators can help students move to a new phase is by including time for reflection and building in guided metacognitive activities.

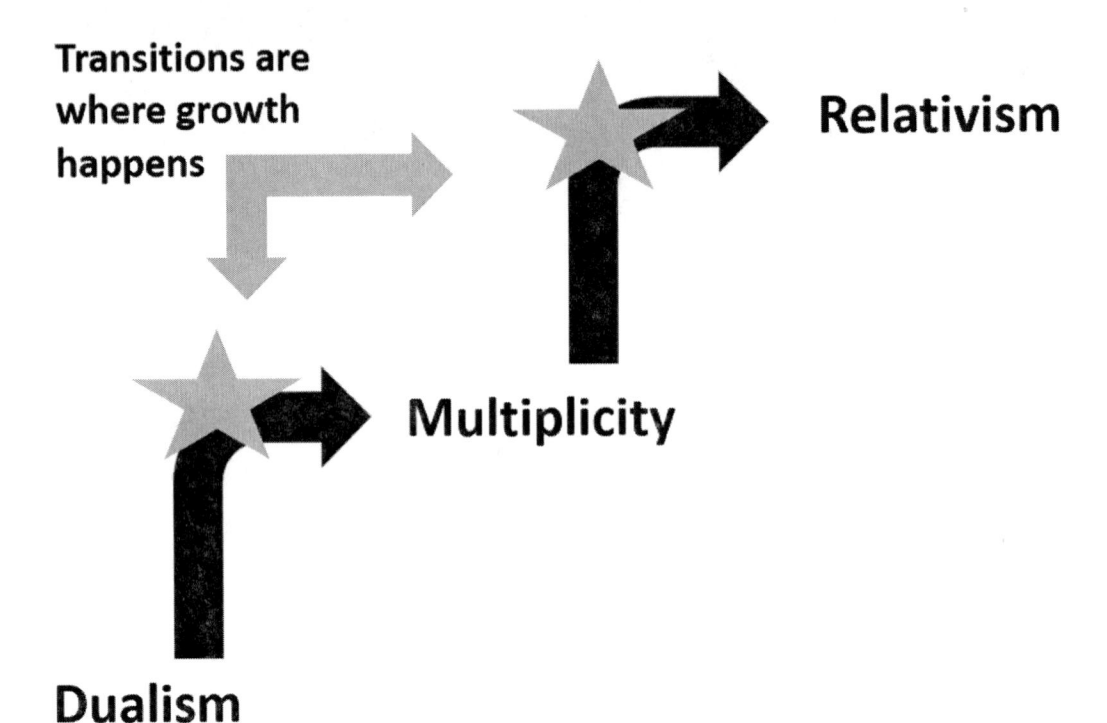

Figure 2.2. Intellectual development transition points

Transition points can be times that are filled with anxiety. Thinking about the world in a different way can leave some people feeling unmoored and uncertain about where they belong. In addition to feeling anxious, students at transition points may also feel apathetic, cynical, or depressed (Perry 1997). While providing prompts to encourage students to think in new ways is important, providing safe spaces and an empathetic recognition that growth is challenging is an equally important responsibility for instructors and librarians.

Perry's theory focuses on students while they are in college and observes how they transition between stages within an academic context. But transitions can happen in other contexts as well. Situations that present a conflict or a challenge can also encourage growth if support is present to make that transition. Transitional phases can be prompted by travel to another country, by significant interactions with a new partner's family members, or because of a new job. People don't need to attend college to undergo intellectual development, but the conflicts and challenges that students encounter in college are common triggers for intellectual development (Long 2012).

Putting Perry's Intellectual and Ethical Development Theory in Context

Perry's work on intellectual and ethical development has important implications for those of us who support and work with students, particularly in an academic setting. However, some caveats should be noted about Perry's theory. As mentioned earlier, Perry's interviews were done primarily at Harvard with white, male students. Some white, female students were interviewed at Radcliffe, but few of their interviews were used in validating the theory. Not only was Perry's demographic pool extremely restrictive in terms of gender and racial diversity, but also the students who attended Harvard in the mid-twentieth century also represented an extremely narrow geographic and socioeconomic spectrum. Later researchers try to address this lack of diversity in Perry's work and have sought to expand this theory to more diverse contexts (Evans et al. 2010).

Another important factor to keep in mind is that Perry's interviews took place at a particular time in history. When Perry later interviewed a different student cohort in 1970, he found that those students were at different stages as compared to the students he initially interviewed in the 1950s and 1960s. Global events were shaping the way those students interpreted information and authority in very different ways. Perry did note the importance of considering these environmental impacts, but he asserted that while certain phases may happen at different times for different students, overall the Intellectual and Ethical Development Theory still provides relevant insights into the changing way students interpret what is happening in the world around them as they progress through college (Perry 1970).

Applying Intellectual Development Phases to the Library Context

Now that you have an understanding of Perry's intellectual development phases and the importance of the transition points between these phases, it is time to think about how these principles can be applied in library settings. Student affairs professionals use Perry's Intellectual and Ethical Development Theory to design programs such as service learning experiences or writing center workshops focused on plagiarism. Through these programs, student affairs professionals seek to give students the opportunity to stretch their initial beliefs and values (Long 2012). Janice Sauer discusses ways that intellectual development principles can help librarians and asserts that Perry's theory provides librarians with "just the kind of framework necessary for designing a program that will work with the developmental pattern of the undergraduate instead of, as we have so often done in the past, against it" (1995, 145). Before delving into ways to use Perry's theory in the library, it is worth considering a cautionary note from Perry that echoes Sauer's sentiments. When designing programs or instruction based on principles of intellectual development, Perry states, "It's not that we need to 'get' students to develop." Rather, he says we should design our curriculum and pedagogical approaches to "invite, encourage, challenge, and support students in such development" (1997, 79).

Learning more about students and respecting the diverse array of intellectual development phases they represent matches up well with many librarians' ethics of putting the learner first and supporting them in the various ways they learn and develop. This section will focus on how librarians can use lessons from Perry's theory in reference, instruction, and outreach. See the box below to help spark your thinking about additional examples of where you have encountered examples of dualism, multiplicity, or relativism in your library context.

> ## INTELLECTUAL DEVELOPMENT PHASE EXAMPLES IN THE LIBRARY
>
> **Dualism**
> Students say . . .
>
> - When is this due?
> - What database should I use?
> - I just can't find the right keywords.
> - My teacher said that we can't use *Wikipedia*.
> - My teacher won't give us any clear directions on what sources to use.
> - I use Ebsco because that's what I used in high school.
>
> **Multiplicity**
> Students say . . .
>
> - I never look at the source. It doesn't really matter where it comes from. The source doesn't matter; content is what I am looking for.
> - The other grad students in my department all use Zotero, so I use it too.
> - I just need a few sources to back up my opinions.
> - I have a system for taking notes that works pretty well for me.
>
> **Relativism**
> Students say . . .
>
> - Because I'm searching in the Web of Science database, I'm not too worried about who wrote this. It's a database for scholarly journals, so I'm not concerned that it's like *Wikipedia* or something like that.
> - Who is the audience for this?
> - A highly cited paper may not be the most relevant one for my project.
> - How do I look outside of my discipline for other perspectives?

Reference Consultations and Intellectual Development

Interactions with students at the reference desk and in-depth, one-on-one research consultations provide many opportunities for observing students at different stages of intellectual development. Students who come to the reference desk are often hurried and stressed out. They may have tried many alternative routes for addressing their questions before coming to you. In these situations of stress and frustration, students can often reveal much about themselves in a short period of time. Also, because reference interactions are short, often onetime encounters, these interactions can leave librarians feeling as if they haven't done enough to support students (see the Real-Life Reference Example in the box below). This section will look at how librarians who do reference work can interact with students in ways that are appropriate for their intellectual development stage; will offer suggestions for structuring research consultations to help students at transition points; and will discuss the value librarians can provide as safe sources of assistance for all students.

REAL-LIFE REFERENCE EXAMPLE

The student approached the reference desk with a couple of her friends. The student said, "I'm doing my paper on how grunge represents the 90s and I need one more source that will give me a couple of quotes." We looked through [several search tools]. I felt pressure because the student kept emphasizing finding quotes, and her friends looked bored. I sent her a couple of citations; but I felt totally inadequate.

—Erin Hvizdak, Washington State University Libraries, personal communication, October 22, 2015

Dualism

Recognizing and respecting the intellectual development stage of your learners helps you present information in a way that encourages learners to be more receptive to that information. Learners at the dualism phase are usually looking for right answers and want you, as an authority figure, either to give them that information or to tell them which sources are authoritative. One way to help learners at this phase is by making sure the information you provide, either verbally or in print, is clear. Learners at the dualism phase are not looking for lengthy descriptions with extraneous information about the history of the source or alternative methods of arriving at the answer. Focus on giving explanations that are brief and to the point.

During the dualism phase, learners also want reassurances that the source they chose or the search tool they used is the best tool. Let students know how you chose the sources and tools you did during a reference interaction, and use language that signals how you determined the authority of the tool or source. For example, a signal phrase can be as simple as saying, "I chose to begin our search in Academic Search Premier because it has a lot of scholarly articles written by researchers on a range of current topics." Noting that this search tool contains scholarly articles is an important cue to the learners. They can use that information to help determine authority when doing another search in the future.

While you may have little control at the reference desk over what sources an instructor requires for the final research project, you can suggest background sources that are more appropriate for the learners' intellectual phase. Authoritative secondary or tertiary sources that compile information in a more digestible format for novice researchers may be more appropriate for students in the dualism phase (Jackson 2008). Sources such as encyclopedias, government websites, or research updates provide the clear authority for learners at this stage without the more complex disciplinary language they may not yet be equipped to evaluate (see table 2.1). While students may not be able to cite sources such as an encyclopedia in their final project, reference librarians can explain the value of beginning their research with these types of sources.

Presenting information in a stage-appropriate way during reference interactions most importantly relies on modeling behaviors that learners can adopt themselves. In summary, some of the ways you can help learners at the dualism stage are by providing

- clear explanations,
- brief directions,

Table 2.1. Suggested source types based on intellectual development phase

PHASE	SUGGESTED SOURCES
Dualism	Encyclopedias or other reference sources Research updates or news Secondary source books (e.g., popular science) Government websites
Multiplicity	Review articles Editorials Blog posts Research updates or news Government and nonprofit websites Primary sources (e.g., from historical disciplines)
Relativism	Original research articles Conference proceedings Government websites Scholarly monographs Primary sources Raw data

- authoritative background source suggestions,
- and signals revealing how authority is determined.

While reference desk interactions are usually brief and rely on quick modeling of search strategies, scheduled one-on-one reference consultations allow librarians to pair search strategy modeling with opportunities for learners to transition to a new intellectual phase. Reflection prompts and questions that encourage learners to consider new ways of thinking help initiate that transition process. Many college-age students are required to find and use peer-reviewed articles as evidence for research-based assignments. Students who are in the dualism phase likely view the authority of peer-reviewed articles in black and white. Up to this point, they may have learned a simplistic version of how the peer-review process works and may believe that peer-reviewed articles are free from bias, and that the information in peer-reviewed articles always provides authoritative evidence. Students may now be ready to learn that peer-reviewed articles are part of a broader scholarly conversation made up of varying viewpoints and a shifting understanding of what constitutes authoritative evidence. Guiding questions in a reference interaction with someone on the edge of the dualism phase could examine the background of the authors from a variety of papers on a similar topic, how these different authors in the same discipline agree and disagree, and whether there are people outside of the scholarly community who are also interested in this topic (see table 2.2). Exploring these questions together in a one-on-one research consultation allows students to consider other sources of authority and that authority may sometimes be situational.

Multiplicity

Learners at the multiplicity phase increasingly rely on their own opinions and ideas as an important source of authority. However, they are becoming open to seeking out opinions and insight from a wider range of sources, including their peers. They are also less inclined

Table 2.2. Research consultation prompts based on intellectual development phases for an example library research scenario

PHASE	LIBRARY RESEARCH CONSULTATION EXAMPLE	TRANSITION PROMPTS
Dualism	A student is looking for facts using peer-reviewed articles for the first part of their research assignment. The student assumes all peer-reviewed articles contain correct information that can be automatically trusted because researchers aren't biased.	• What shared perspectives do the authors have? • What do the authors disagree about? • Why might they disagree? • Besides people in the scholarly community, who else is interested in this topic? • Where could we find information about what other interested parties are saying?
Multiplicity	The second part of the research assignment requires the student to do her own survey of other college students. The student chooses a topic she feels strongly about. The results are quite different than what the student has read in the peer-reviewed literature.	• What do you know about the researchers' academic training and experience? • How do the methods and sample sizes compare among the research studies you are examining? • Do researchers need to include all of their data or background ideas? • How do you think they choose what to include?
Relativism	The third part of the research assignment asks the student to synthesize her own research and research done by others in the discipline and to include an analysis of limitations and future directions the research could take.	• When would it be appropriate to include nonscholarly works in your paper? • When would it be inappropriate to include scholarly works in your paper? • How does peer review or input from others in the field impact a research paper? • How quickly do you think new ideas, theories, or ways of understanding emerge in your field? • How will you decide what data and information to use in your paper? • How has your thinking about this research area changed since you started this project?

to categorize one type of information as qualitatively more valuable or important than another. Students at this phase have had some experience both with college and with doing academic research, and they are beginning to understand that instructors don't just want regurgitated facts but rather want students to interpret and present their information using some of the conventions they have learned in their discipline.

Modeling search strategies at the reference desk is a valuable way to meet learners' needs at the multiplicity phase. Because they are willing to explore other sources of authority, capitalize on that interest and demonstrate a broader range of search tools and source types. Go beyond the basics of a discovery tool or broad scholarly database, and show students in the multiplicity phase subject-specific databases. Or show them scholarly information aggregators such as ScienceBlogs, Research Blogging, or ScienceSeeker to expand their view of where and how scholarly conversations take place. Editorials in scholarly journals can be a valuable source for demonstrating how scholars form their opinions (see table 2.1 for more source suggestions). Learners at the multiplicity phase should have a better understanding of how keywords work and that different audiences may use language differently. Point out subject headings, thesauri, and synonyms to illustrate how experts use language in various ways depending on their audience.

Learners at the multiplicity phase will still appreciate clear, brief explanations, as well as signals that distinguish how authority is conveyed. But there are new approaches you can use when providing reference assistance to learners at the multiplicity phase. In summary, these approaches include

- demonstrating a wider range of search tools, including more discipline-specific tools;
- showing sources that reveal broader scholarly opinions, including blogs and editorials; and
- discussing how keywords change depending on the audience.

Because learners in the multiplicity phase are learning how to rely on themselves for evidence, instructors can build on this reliance by asking students to engage in their own original research activities. However, some confusion may arise when student researchers begin to compare their work to that of other, more experienced researchers. Here are some examples of more in-depth research consultation prompts to encourage learners at the multiplicity phase to transition to new ways of thinking:

- Ask learners to explore how more established researchers gained their expertise.
- Encourage a more nuanced examination of methods and sample sizes so students can compare and contrast their techniques to those of other researchers.
- Ask learners to reflect on what ideas are actually included in a researcher's final report so students can begin to learn how to synthesize ideas into a format acceptable in their disciplinary context (see table 2.2 for more ideas).

Relativism

Learners at the relativism phase should be more confident in their ability to understand when to use different search tools and source types in their own research processes. As these learners are confronted with a new range of sources and data types, they will need to determine how to prioritize and synthesize information from all these sources. Learners at this stage will use the information at their disposal differently depending on the context. For example, when asked to create a presentation for a nonscholarly audience, such as a local nonprofit, they should be able to present information that is engaging and appropriate for that audience. When asked to write a report for an audience of public officials, they should be able to include and cite data and statistics to make a compelling argument.

Reference desk support for learners at the relativism phase will most frequently arise as learners are trying out new tools outside of their typical disciplinary domain. While they may be able to transfer some of their underlying knowledge from their own field about how to choose search tools, how to navigate source types, and how to determine if evidence comes from an authoritative source, they made need some insights into how information is conveyed, organized, and accessed in an unfamiliar context. For example, a food scientist looking for patent information for the first time may need direction on how patent searching works. Or a marine biology student may need some help finding census data to present to policymakers. Helping learners cross disciplinary boundaries and expand their understanding of what constitutes a quality source in an unfamiliar discipline is an important role that librarians can play for learners at the relativism stage (see table 2.1 for suggested source types). In addition, reference librarians can suggest tools that help researchers determine the value or ranking of journals or articles. These tools include altmetrics, the H-index, and *Journal Citation Reports*. While none of these tools are perfect, they provide researchers with a mechanism for establishing a benchmark for the authority of research or evidence in a field.

In summary, reference practices that support learners at the relativism phase include

- demonstrating search tools and sources from multidisciplinary contexts;
- signaling how different research communities establish authority; and
- suggesting tools for evaluating scholarly impact.

Learners who are at the relativism phase are becoming more comfortable evaluating which source is more authoritative and which sources make more sense depending on the context. Nonetheless, as learners initially enter this phase, practice and explicit reflection are needed to clarify how decisions about prioritizing sources and choosing what information to report are made. Examples of research consultation prompts for learners at this phase include questions about the appropriateness of using either scholarly or nonscholarly sources depending on the learner's disciplinary context. Learners at the relativism phase can also benefit from a discussion about the effectiveness of the peer-review process, how the process of peer-review impacts the speed with which new information is shared in their field, and what some alternatives to the traditional peer-review process might be. Finally, learners at this stage can benefit from working with a librarian who can serve as a neutral sounding board for their reflections about how their thinking has evolved and grown since they started their research project (see table 2.2).

Library as a Safe Space

Libraries are traditionally known for their role as safe, community-gathering spaces. Learners can come to the library and ask a range of questions, including questions that are immediately relevant to library topics and those that range further afield. The range of questions asked reflects learners' view of librarians as relatively safe and neutral information authorities. An analysis of reference desk interactions at an academic library found that 47 percent of the questions were non-research related. When reflecting on their findings, the study authors noted that part of the role of librarians may be to help students learn the new culture of being in college and how to ask for help from authority figures (Grallo, Chalmers, and Baker 2012).

While learners may need more assistance adapting to a new culture during the dualism phase, as learners transition through the intellectual development phases, their need for safe people and spaces to go to for information remains constant. As you observe trends and issues learners are facing, use this opportunity to connect with other stakeholders and communicate with them about these issues. For example, if students are consistently having problems with the campus learning management system (LMS), take the time to pass this information along to the relevant IT group on your campus. Or if you encounter many graduate students who have difficulties navigating the advisor-advisee relationship, talk with your graduate school to see if you can collaborate to create a support system for advisors and advisees.

Librarians often bring a more service-driven, human approach to their work that learners may find lacking in other encounters with city government or campus offices.

One way to build on the idea of librarians as a safe connecting point is through the use of personal librarian programs. Several large academic libraries use personal librarian programs to make an initially intimidating system such as the library feel more approachable. Students can receive e-mails from their personal librarian letting them know about library updates; they can meet with their personal librarian for research help; and their personal librarian can connect them with other campus services. Examples of universities with personal librarian programs include Yale University, the University of Iowa, Drexel University, and the University of North Carolina at Chapel Hill. Librarians may have once sat behind large reference desks that conveyed a certain type of authority, but librarians are now breaking down those walls. By paying attention to their learners' intellectual development phases, librarians can provide even more relevant assistance at the learners' point of need.

Library Instruction and Intellectual Development

Librarians who teach students either as guest lecturers in one-shot sessions or as instructors for term-long classes have more time to observe and determine the intellectual development phases of their students. Instruction librarians also have more opportunities for tailoring an instruction experience that appropriately matches students' intellectual development phases. This section will build on the suggestions given above for reference librarians. Because many of the suggestions for sources to use and ideas for helping learners transition to new phases are the same for reference and instruction librarians, this section will focus on examples of instructional strategies and activities that are appropriate for various learners' intellectual development phases.

Dualism

Learners at the dualism phase are still learning how to navigate the information landscape, particularly in an academic context, and are unlikely to be aware that authorities in a field may hold somewhat different opinions or may approach problems in different ways. Because learners in the dualism phase still categorize information and sources of authority as black and white, these learners will be more inclined to see these academic differences of opinion as a rejection of a theory or idea. Instead, researchers may be trying to make a theory stronger by providing as many diverse perspectives as possible. An example learning objective and assignment for learners in the dualism phase inspired by Rebecca Jackson's (2008) mapping of the intellectual development phases to the ACRL Information Literacy Competency Standards is described next to help prompt your thinking about ways you could meet the needs of your learners.

The example one-shot session in table 2.3 introduces learners to the way scholarly conversations happen by asking them to find an academic debate that is currently underway on a topic the student is interested in and then to summarize the viewpoints represented in that debate. Students may rely on sources such as *Wikipedia*, which includes a "Talk" tab showing the discussion that goes into creating an article. Or they could explore research news sites such as ScienceDaily or EurekAlert! that cover current research topics.

Several key instructional strategies are important for learners in the dualism phase. Just as with reference interactions, clarity is important for these learners. Make sure either paper or web-based versions of the assignment directions are clear and to the point. Another important instructional strategy is to first model the behaviors you want students

Table 2.3. Instructional strategies for library sessions based on intellectual development phase

PHASE	EXAMPLE LEARNING OUTCOME	INSTRUCTIONAL STRATEGIES	ACTIVITIES
Dualism	Identify an academic debate in the student's major in order to write a short summary of an issue that is still developing and is important in their field.	• Provide clarity. • Model behaviors first. • Use preselected examples and discussion prompts. • Include time for individual feedback.	• Use clear directions—verbal and written. • Model how to find topics under debate, include explicit explanations of choices made. • Use the Cephalonian method to prompt students to read statements on different sides of an example topic. • Work individually with all students on their topics to make sure they understand the assignment. • Use the muddiest point paper exercise.
Multiplicity	Find and read several academic and nonacademic sources on the same topic in order to present a comparison of the range of arguments on that topic.	• Students try the activity first. • Model key behaviors second. • Students share in pairs. • Students practice with a preselected example.	• Ask students to work in pairs. First one participant looks for academic sources, and the other looks for nonacademic sources. Debrief with each other on where they looked and then switch roles. • Model reading a source to find the key argument, include explicit explanations of signposts and signal words you noticed within the source. • Have students practice reading assigned example sources to find the key arguments. Document the signal words the authors used. • Do a misconception/preconception check.
Relativism	Find and read several academic and nonacademic sources that include data, and discuss the same topic in order to write a synthesis paper that includes original data on that topic.	• Students try the activity first. • Provide minimal instructor modeling. • Students learn in pairs. • Students learn from each other. • Ask more complex questions about source validity and disciplinary differences.	• Ask students to work in pairs. Assign students example charts with raw data from a scholarly and nonscholarly source. Ask them to report back to the group on a summary of the key data, and share one technique for reading charts. • Model any missing techniques for reading charts. • Students review the charts again in pairs, and report back about what other data could have been collected or may have been left out. • Look for original research articles that might fill in the gaps in the data. • Use a mind map.

to adopt. Before asking students to find a topic and explore sources, demonstrate how you would approach the assignment. Talk through the decisions you make, and choose realistic examples. Depending on how far along students are in the dualism phase, it may be best to skip the topic selection stage and instead provide them with preassigned topics. Allowing students to explore topics under debate that you have identified, without the pressure of choosing a topic in a field they are not yet familiar with, will help students more readily recognize appropriate topics in future assignments. Because learners in the dualism phase still rely on outside authorities for confirmation, build in enough time to provide individual feedback on their work.

A classroom activity that may be particularly appropriate for learners in the dualism phase is the Cephalonian method (Morgan and Davies 2008). The Cephalonian method uses preprepared questions or scenarios so that students can focus on the content of the questions rather than on coming up with their own questions. In this activity the librarian distributes the prepared questions, which are usually color-coded, to students, and then when a particular color is called out, students read aloud the prepared question. For the academic debate example, the librarian could demonstrate how scholars make arguments in an academic debate by providing students with statements representing alternate sides of the same topic. When called upon, students could stage a mock debate by reading the statements they were given. This active learning technique gets students involved and models how scholars communicate without putting pressure on students to immediately find their own examples.

A useful wrap-up activity is a quick reflective writing exercise such as the muddiest point or a one-minute reflection paper (Angelo and Cross 1993). These reflection exercises ask students to either write about something they are still confused about (the muddiest point) or what they learned in class (one-minute reflection). These quick assessment activities serve both the learners and the instructor. The learner benefits from pausing to reflect on what they do or don't know. The instructor gains insights into what students have learned or are still confused about.

In summary, some instructional strategies that are appropriate for learners at the dualism phase include the following:

- Providing clear instructions
- Modeling behaviors before asking students to demonstrate the behavior
- Creating a safe space by providing preselected topics or example scenarios
- Giving individual feedback
- Providing opportunity for reflection

Finally, as learners transition to the next phase, a key strategy is to avoid library assignments or exercises that only expect single, right answers. As Sauer (1995) points out, oversimplified exercises that remove all elements of complexity won't help true learning happen.

Multiplicity

Learners in the multiplicity phase not only see themselves as a source of authority but also see many other voices as potential sources of authority. Learners at this phase will be less likely to categorize a source as authoritative simply because it comes from a preapproved list of sources or from a database that typically contains scholarly sources (see the Real-Life Instruction Example in the box below). However, learners at this phase may need some prompting to look outside of the circle of sources they are already familiar with. The example learning objective and assignment described next provides learners with the opportunity to engage with a variety of source types and to compare and contrast the evidence from each of these source types (see table 2.3).

REAL-LIFE INSTRUCTION EXAMPLE

Students were assigned to fill out discussion modules in Canvas [the learning management system] after a library session. One student questioned the utility of searching for background sources and books, and said the same types of sources could be found online.

—Chelsea Nesvig, University of Washington, Bothell Campus, personal communication, October 22, 2015

This example one-shot library session builds on the previous assignment for learners at the dualism phase. Again, learners engage with a topic of academic debate. However, in this assignment learners must find and read several academic and nonacademic sources on the topic under debate. Ideally, the topic would relate to the learner's major field of study. After finding and reading a range of sources, learners must compare and contrast the evidence used in those sources. Students may use some of the same sources suggested for learners in the dualism phase such as research news websites and government websites. However, they may need specific suggestions of where to look for new sources of both academic and nonacademic conversations. For example, suggesting specific nonprofit websites or web aggregators they haven't previously encountered can provide students with new avenues to explore. Students should also be encouraged to begin using source types scholars in their field might use such as review articles or primary sources. Students will likely need to be directed to these sources, especially because these source types often require the use of specialized search tools or search strategies.

The instructional strategies for learners at the multiplicity phase give students an opportunity to build on their existing expertise and to do more independent exploration. Instead of beginning by modeling the exercise for the students, provide brief, clear instructions, and ask students to try some searching on their own first. While they are exploring, walk around the room and observe what tools they try and what problems they may be running into. After students have had a chance to explore some search tools and sources, model some specific behaviors you would like them to try out. For example, if you see that students already know how to access databases in their discipline to find scholarly articles but that no one has located any review articles, you could demonstrate how to find that specific article type. Scaffolding the class time based on a recognition of the experience students already have can make students more receptive to new techniques you present.

Another instructional strategy is to ask students to share responses and observations in pairs first before sharing their responses with the entire class. The think-pair-share activity allows students to develop confidence in their ideas, gather insights from their peers, and finally demonstrate their understanding to the class. Another pair-based activity is to ask one member of the pair to find a scholarly source and the other member to find a nonscholarly source on the same topic. Students can then discuss with each other how they found their sources and what evidence their source used, and then they can compare the two sources. Next, the pairs can switch roles and take turns looking for the source type they have not yet explored. As with the exercise used for learners in the dualism phase, depending on how much time you have, and how much experience students have in their field of study, it might be helpful to provide preselected topics so that students can put most of their energy into finding, reading, and comparing a variety of sources.

For students in the multiplicity phase, a useful wrap-up assessment activity is the misconception/preconception check (Angelo and Cross 1993). This exercise encourages students to reflect on how their thinking on a particular topic has changed during the class period. Students write briefly about what they thought about a certain topic at the beginning of the class and what they think now. For example, you could ask students how they viewed evidence from nonacademic sources at the beginning of class and what they think now.

In summary, some instructional strategies that are appropriate for learners at the multiplicity phase include the following:

- Suggesting new source types
- Allowing independent exploration
- Modeling specific, scaffolded behaviors
- Working first in pairs
- Valuing their input and expertise
- Providing opportunities for reflection

Some other interesting instructional activities and strategies appropriate for learners at the multiplicity phase have been written about elsewhere. Jackson (2008) describes learners at the multiplicity phase as able to understand the variety of factors that go into retrieving search results from a search tool like Google. An exercise exploring how Google search results are different based on location, past search histories, purchasing habits, and the search engine optimization savvy of the web developer can lead to a discussion about the economics and social factors that go into determining relevancy rankings. Maio and Shaughnessy (2012) use a framework of collaboration with learners at the multiplicity phase because of the framework's emphasis on learning from other people's experiences. In their plagiarism workshop geared toward student leaders, instead of only sharing the experiences of the workshop leaders, participants also share their experiences. Because of the use of this technique, the workshop leaders found student engagement in their own development greatly increased. These examples illustrate ways to engage students in more complex understandings of authority, and the importance of valuing learner input.

Relativism

Learners at the relativism phase are increasingly able to prioritize opinions based on the evidence presented. Additionally, they take into account the context for opinions as they try to establish how to use information. Because they have had practice interpreting information from an increasingly wide variety of source types, they know when to use information for different audiences. As noted in the section on reference librarians, learners at this phase may need to work in multidisciplinary areas and may still need help navigating sources they haven't encountered in their previous work such as raw data or primary sources. The example learning objective and assignment described next encourages students to build on the skills they have and to collaborate with others to use information in a more hands-on way (see table 2.3).

This example one-shot exercise continues with the idea of looking at an academically debated topic from multiple angles. Learners at the relativism phase should have had practice reading and interpreting both academic and nonacademic sources. This exercise asks learners to explore the data presented in original research so students can draw their own conclusions about the evidence presented. Again, for this exercise students are encouraged to use both academic and nonacademic sources. However, both sources need to include graphs, tables, or some type of data the students can analyze. Students may use a broad range of sources including government websites or reports but should now expand their repertoire to include original research articles, conference proceedings (if appropriate for their field), data sets, or scholarly monographs. Unless students are new to this particular field of study, guidance on how to find these source types should be fairly minimal.

As with learners at the multiplicity phase, learners at the relativism phase should be given brief, clear instructions, and then they can search on their own. If the librarian notices problems or issues while observing students trying to find sources, brief explanations can be given, but the need for instructor modeling should be much more minimal. Instead, the work of the instructor is to provide assignments and questions for reflection that are complex enough to engage these learners. Work in pairs is still appropriate for these learners, as interactions with a peer will encourage a broader range of perspectives. An example task for the pairs could be to explore how they determine the validity of the sources they are using and how data is used differently depending on the disciplinary context.

An example activity for this class is to examine data from both scholarly and nonscholarly sources in pairs. Depending on how much time you have, either preselect the figures and tables or have students choose their own data sets. Students should explain the main point of the charts to each other, provide alternative explanations for the information presented in the charts, and determine whether or not more data needs to be collected or presented to convince them of the validity of the data. Students can then search for other sources that can fill in any remaining information gaps.

Because of the complexity of synthesizing information from a wide range of sources, students could illustrate the connections and gaps they have found in their data with a concept or mind map. Asking students to draw a quick mind-map sketch of the main concepts they have encountered can help learners see new connections between ideas and allows you to see what they have learned.

In summary, some instruction strategies for learners at the relativism phase include the following:

- Showing how to access unfamiliar source types
- Providing challenging assignments and exercises
- Minimal modeling, only as needed
- Encouraging work in pairs to showcase diverse viewpoints
- Valuing their input and expertise
- Giving opportunities for reflection and synthesis

Learners at the relativism phase are active participants in their own learning. Margaret Weaver (2013) recommends shifting our thinking from viewing students as people to be taught at to viewing students as people to collaborate with, who can create and deliver content. Learners at the relativism phase will appreciate this enhanced responsibility and the ability to demonstrate their expertise. Specific domain expertise is still needed for learners to successfully navigate more complex information landscapes. However, Perry

(1997) argues that the intellectual habits of mind learners develop can be transferred to new domains learners encounter.

Library Outreach and Intellectual Development

Library outreach is still a relatively new area, but outreach activities can be used to showcase different views of authority that are meaningful for learners at a range of intellectual development phases. Because learners interact with outreach activities in a less formal way, often without a librarian present, the activities described next are not divided up by intellectual development phase. Instead, learners can choose to be stimulated or engaged at a level of their own choosing.

Library outreach activities often contain interactive elements that invite the participant to become a creator. As a result, these activities can shift the idea of an authority from only belonging to experts to including anyone who wants to try and make something. This idea can be particularly meaningful for learners transitioning between the dualism and multiplicity phases. An example of an outreach activity that includes hands-on making activities open to all learners is a Maker Faire. Maker Faires are frequently hosted at public libraries. Participants at Maker Faires use both new technologies such as 3-D printing and older technologies such as soldering metals. The popularity of these events is growing as participants seek to try out new tools and embrace the idea that they too can be a creator. Crafternoons are another example of an outreach program that focuses on making things. Both public and academic libraries host Crafternoons to showcase craft-based activities such as paper piecing, snowflake making, and embroidery. At the New York Public Library, their Crafternoon event wraps up with a presentation of the work each participant has created.

Outreach activities can also showcase voices whose authority is not often recognized in our society. Book displays featuring authors from traditionally underrepresented groups, or books by authors from different countries, can help learners contemplate how our society chooses whose voices are heard. Posters or banners that accompany the book displays highlighting alternative voices to consider and questioning how authority is determined can help prompt learners at the multiplicity and relativism phases to look for new sources of authority and ways to use evidence to make meaning from a broad variety of sources.

Key Points

Development is a continuous process, and learners need safe spaces in which to explore and grow. Understanding the range of intellectual development phases of your learners can inform the way you provide reference assistance, design instruction sessions, and promote outreach activities. Here are some key points to take away:

- As learners progress through the intellectual development phases, their understanding of authority shifts from seeing authority as belonging to a few individuals to seeing authority as belonging to anyone with an opinion and to seeing authority as being determined by the quality of the evidence and the specific context.
- Reference interactions can provide opportunities for suggesting sources appropriate for the learner's intellectual development phase. Questions that prompt exploration of new ideas can help learners transition to new phases.

- Instruction sessions that are appropriate for learners' intellectual phases use instructional strategies such as modeling how to think as a researcher and reflective activities that encourage learners to participate in their own intellectual development.
- Outreach activities provide learners with the opportunity to see themselves as individuals with the authority to create, as well as to become aware of voices that typically aren't given authority in our society.

Now that you understand the value of using Perry's Intellectual and Ethical Development Theory in your work as a librarian, you are ready to explore some alternative theories of intellectual development. Chapter 3 will guide you through an intellectual development theory based on a more diverse range of learners and will discuss ways to encourage development when dealing with more difficult, real-world problems.

References

ACRL (Association of College and Research Libraries). 2016. "Framework for Information Literacy for Higher Education." January 11. http://www.ala.org/.

Angelo, Thomas A., and K. Patricia Cross. 1993. *Classroom Assessment Techniques: A Handbook for College Teachers*. 2nd ed. Jossey-Bass Higher and Adult Education Series. San Francisco: Jossey-Bass.

Evans, Nancy J., Deanna S. Forney, Florence M. Guido, Lori D. Patton, and Kristen A. Renn. 2010. *Student Development in College: Theory, Research, and Practice*. 2nd ed. Jossey-Bass Higher and Adult Education Series. San Francisco: Jossey-Bass.

Grallo, Jacqui D., Mardi Chalmers, and Pamela G. Baker. 2012. "How Do I Get a Campus ID? The Other Role of the Academic Library in Student Retention and Success." *Reference Librarian* 53 (2): 182–93. doi:10.1080/02763877.2011.618787.

Jackson, Rebecca. 2008. "Information Literacy and Its Relationship to Cognitive Development and Reflective Judgement." *New Directions for Student Services*, no. 114 (Summer): 47–61. doi:10.1002/tl.316.

Long, Dallas. 2012. "Theories and Models of Student Development." In *Environments for Student Growth and Development: Libraries and Student Affairs in Collaboration*, edited by Lisa Janicke Hinchliffe and Melissa Autumn Wong, 41–56. Chicago: Association of College and Research Libraries.

Maio, Natalie, and Kathryn Shaughnessy. 2012. "Promoting Collaborative LEADers in the St. John's University Community." In *Environments for Student Growth and Development: Libraries and Student Affairs in Collaboration*, edited by Lisa Janicke Hinchliffe and Melissa Autumn Wong, 87–100. Chicago: Association of College and Research Libraries.

Morgan, Nigel, and Linda Davies. 2008. "How Cephalonia Can Conquer the World (or at the Very Least Your Students!)." In *Practical Pedagogy for Library Instructors: 17 Innovative Strategies to Improve Student Learning*, edited by Douglas Cook and Ryan Sittler, 20–29. Chicago: Association of College and Research Libraries.

Perry, William G. 1970. *Forms of Intellectual and Ethical Development in the College Years: A Scheme*. New York: Holt, Rinehart and Winston.

Perry, William G., Jr. 1997. "Cognitive and Ethical Growth: The Making of Meaning." In *College Student Development and Academic Life*, edited by Karen Arnold and Ilda Carreiro King, 48–87. Contemporary Higher Education: International Issues for the Twenty-First Century. New York: Garland.

Sauer, Janice A. 1995. "Conversation 101: Process, Development and Collaboration." In *Information for a New Age: Redefining the Librarian*, edited by Lois M. Pausch, 135–51. Englewood, CO: Libraries Unlimited.

Weaver, Margaret. 2013. "Student Journey Work: A Review of Academic Library Contributions to Student Transition and Success." *New Review of Academic Librarianship* 19 (2): 101–24. doi:10.1080/13614533.2013.800754.

CHAPTER 3

Making Sense of Difficult Problems

IN THIS CHAPTER

▷ Understanding how learners face ill-structured and uncomfortable information questions

▷ Providing learners with strategies for evaluating evidence based on contextual cues

▷ Modeling ways of thinking through tough questions

HAVE YOU EVER OBSERVED STUDENTS in an instruction session clinging to topics they've used before and unwilling to research new areas, especially if they encounter ideas that contradict their point of view? Have you ever struggled to convince students at the reference desk that alternative keywords might be needed to broaden a topic beyond an overly narrow starting point? Or have you ever watched advanced learners quickly adapt a search tool you demonstrated into their workflow, exploring features for themselves that you didn't even introduce?

These positive and negative questions and experiences illustrate some of the more complex intellectual development behaviors learners—including librarians—express as they try to solve more difficult problems and take responsibility for their own learning experiences. The last chapter introduced Perry's Intellectual and Ethical Development Theory as a way to understand how learners approach intellectual challenges related to determining authority and making meaning from varied types of evidence based on their stage of intellectual development. Knowing that learners progress through different developmental stages and process information accordingly explains some of the variability in behavior that librarians observe in their practice on the reference desk, in the classroom, and when doing outreach. Chapter 2 presented strategies for encouraging learners at different stages of development to think about authority and evidence in new ways and discussed how to translate theory into action.

The model selected for this chapter—the Reflective Judgment Model—was chosen because of the way it builds on earlier intellectual development theories and for its applicability within libraries. Chapter 2 included examples of how librarians could craft services and programs that were appropriate for a wide range of learners based on their developmental stage and also provided transitional opportunities to encourage growth. Instead of focusing on the stages in this intellectual development model, the examples provided in this chapter will focus on the key principles from the Reflective Judgment Model and how librarians can apply those principles within the contexts of reference, instruction, and outreach.

The Reflective Judgment Model explores how learners grapple with questions that don't have clear-cut answers. Many difficult intellectual challenges surround us in our everyday lives. American society is increasingly polarized, and despite a wealth of information available online, people often make the choice (both consciously and subconsciously) to engage only with voices and knowledge that matches their preexisting understanding of the world (Chatman 1999; Mirani 2014; Pariser 2011). While librarians aren't neutral (we're human too!), libraries can serve as a place where diverse ideas and information from a wide range of sources can be shared.

Librarians have the opportunity to prepare learners for many of the intellectual challenges they face. Because librarians have embraced lifelong learning as a core value, librarians are already well positioned to work with learners who are in the middle of dealing with difficult questions (ALA Council 2004). Librarians in a variety of settings can encourage advanced learners to go beyond the mechanics of evaluating information, by modeling how to ask deeper questions so learners can develop their own problem-solving strategies. This chapter will provide practical strategies and activities librarians can use with learners to encourage deeper thinking and opportunities to practice dealing with more complex questions.

Cognitive-Structural Theories Expanded

Chapter 2 introduced cognitive-structural theories—the group of theories that describe how people think, reason, and make decisions. The previous chapter concentrated on one of the seminal theories in the student development field, William Perry's Intellectual and Ethical Development Theory, which was based on high school and traditional college-aged student behaviors. This chapter will continue to use examples from that age group but will also incorporate strategies from a theory that addresses intellectual development challenges that extend later into life. As learners collect a range of experiences and move into the upper stages defined by these models, specific developmental stages become less important as a means for describing learners' behaviors. Instead, this chapter will examine how librarians can assist learners as they face new contexts and make harder decisions.

Beyond the classroom, learners face real-world problems that require advanced strategies for dealing with questions that don't have a single answer. Theories of how learners progressively deal with complicated, real-world problems can help librarians to be more understanding of their learners' needs and to recognize when different approaches may encourage learners to push beyond their comfort zones. The next sections will provide background information for the Reflective Judgment Model so that librarians will be able to expand their ability to adapt intellectual development theories to their contexts.

The Reflective Judgment Model

After Perry introduced his intellectual development theory, other researchers were eager to test this model and discover whether Perry's ideas about how learners develop their thinking over time held true in other contexts. One of the most well-known adaptations examined learner behavior during, and also after, the traditional college-age years. Patricia King, Karen Kitchener, and their research assistants expanded on earlier intellectual development theories by interviewing 1,700 people who were between fourteen and sixty-five years old (King and Kitchener 1994). In addition to performing onetime interviews, they (and their collaborators) also gathered information from longitudinal studies over ten years examining eighty participants. Based on this work, they created the Reflective Judgment Model.

In practice, the Reflective Judgment Model has many similarities to Perry's Intellectual and Ethical Development Theory. The Reflective Judgment Model also has seven stages that learners progress through in a step-wise manner. Just as in Perry's model, these seven stages can be grouped into three main categories (see figure 3.1):

- Prereflective thinking
- Quasi-reflective thinking
- Reflective thinking

In the *prereflective thinking* stage, learners see knowledge as concrete and knowable. During the *quasi-reflective thinking* stage, learners understand there may be multiple answers to complex questions, but they struggle to evaluate all the possible answers and conclude that all answers are equally valid. Learners at the *reflective thinking* stage understand that there are multiple perspectives on many topics and that there are accepted societal or disciplinary standards to help evaluate those perspectives (Rempel, Buck, and Deitering 2013). These categories map closely to Perry's *dualism*, *multiplicity*, and *relativism* phases.

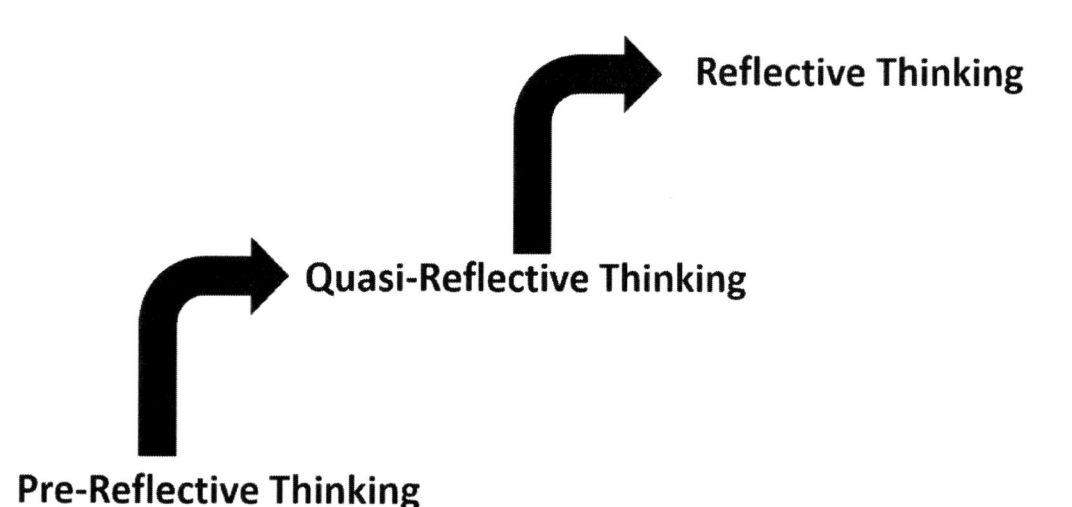

Figure 3.1. Reflective Judgment Model phases of thinking

What makes King and Kitchener's Reflective Judgment Model worth exploring is not that they arrived at similar developmental stages as Perry but rather that the difference in how they arrived at their categories is key to applying this theory to the library context. When conducting their interviews, King and Kitchener focused on what they refer to as "ill-structured problems." They define ill-structured problems as "problems that have no easy or complete solution . . . you may need to come back to them multiple times as you have new information to reframe your understanding" (1994, 11). Some examples of the ill-structured problems they asked their study participants to explore were, "Can you know for sure that the Egyptians built the pyramids without help?" (1994, 144), and how do you view the "objectivity of news reporting" (1994, 107). Some of their ill-structured problems were more discipline specific, but other problems described real-world, societal issues that most people will think about at some point such as pollution, hunger, or inflation.

This description of ill-structured problems likely sounds quite familiar to many librarians. Academic librarians frequently work with first-year students who are learning how to research both sides of an issue for argument papers. (See the Examples of Ill-Structured Problems box for topics librarians commonly encounter when providing reference or instruction sessions for first-year composition courses.) While a student may have chosen an ill-structured problem as a topic, a first-year student who is in the prereflective or quasi-reflective thinking stage will have a very different approach to selecting and using information for examining these problems than would a graduate student who is in the reflective thinking stage. This distinction intuitively makes sense, but it raises the question, what can librarians do to help learners, regardless of their current stage, engage more fully with these hard questions?

EXAMPLES OF ILL-STRUCTURED PROBLEMS FROM FIRST-YEAR RESEARCH PROJECTS

- What is the influence of observing violence in video games in the real world?
- Is the use of iPads in elementary schools an effective teaching tool?
- What is the impact of divorce on children?
- How should communities plan for tsunamis?
- What form of clean energy is best to help address climate change issues?
- Should college athletes receive a salary?
- How have the World War II Japanese internment camps affected U.S. society?

King and Kitchener suggest that it takes practice to use reflective judgment to solve ill-structured, real-world problems. Alternatively, they note that without practice, learners won't develop reflective thinking habits. So, while first-year college students typically progress from stage 3 to stage 5 as seniors (on the seven-point scale), based on their longitudinal studies, King and Kitchener determined that not all learners progress at the same rate and that it is rare for learners to reach stage 7. However, the Reflective Judgment Model is not meant to create an expectation that learners must reach expert status or perfection but instead encourages growth and improvement as learners tackle ill-structured problems in new ways. See the Advanced Learners One-Shot Library Instruction Scenario for a real-life example where a librarian observes how different students tackle an ill-structured question.

ADVANCED LEARNERS
ONE-SHOT LIBRARY INSTRUCTION SCENARIO

To better understand the principles of the Reflective Judgment Model in a real-world context, picture yourself as the librarian in the following scenario. Ask yourself how the Reflective Judgment Model could help you address issues you observe in this class.

You are teaching a one-shot library session for a nutrition science class that contains both upper-division undergraduate students and graduate students. The graduate students have all held professional positions in fields related to health, nutrition, or dietetics. A few of the undergraduate students have had internships, but most of the undergraduates have only done coursework related to their field of study. The class assignment involves a group project where students select a real-life case study with a realistic client profile and history. Students must create a dietary action plan for the client based on original research studies they find using subject databases. Because these are advanced students, the instructor allows them to choose their own groups. She also feels they should already have had practice using academic sources and just wants you to show a few tips on how to use a new database. After presenting some search strategies, you notice that student groups without graduate students seem to finish the project very quickly, whereas groups with graduate students are taking longer and are having involved exchanges about what evidence to use based on nuances presented in the client profile. As you talk with the students, it becomes clear that based on the graduate students' professional experiences, they wanted to explore a broader range of sources of evidence to make sure the dietary action plan best meets the client's unique needs. When you debrief with the instructor, you suggest that some more guided prompts or activities might be useful for those students who have had less experience choosing sources in order to solve a real-life problem.

When faced with an ill-structured, real-world problem, the graduate students responded with a reflective thinking approach by seeking multiple perspectives and a range of types of evidence rather than assuming the scenario could be solved with a single, easy answer. However, many of the undergraduate students needed more concrete guidance to help them consider more sources and to interrogate the questions from different angles.

Similar to Perry's interest in the value of transition points in student development, King and Kitchener (1994) contend that uncomfortable or disconcerting experiences are necessary for stimulating development. The key component to development in the Reflective Judgment Model is the assumption that learners must be active participants in the process of learning and that their background influences shape how they will interpret information. Educators can create environments that encourage stretching experiences (within a safe space) and value learners' prior knowledge. Suggestions and strategies for creating experiences based on ill-structured questions within library settings will be explored next.

Applying the Reflective Judgment Model to the Library Context

The Reflective Judgment Model's key principle is learning to ask important and appropriate questions when faced with ill-structured and uncomfortable problems. A recent Project Information Literacy study focusing on young adults' postcollege information behaviors illustrates the struggles people face when they don't learn how to develop their own questions. Researchers interviewed young adults in the years following college graduation to find out what types of information challenges they were facing and what information supports they used to solve those problems. One of the striking findings from this study was that only 27 percent of the study participants felt that college had prepared them to ask questions and stay motivated as learners. A more engaged learning process that includes guided opportunities to practice dealing with tough issues is needed to help develop those habits (Head 2016). This study has clear implications for librarians who are heavily invested not only in connecting learners with information but also with making sure they are able to use that information. This section will provide practical examples of how librarians can help learners develop the ability to deal with hard questions in reference, instruction, and outreach settings.

Reference Consultations and the Reflective Judgment Model

Reference interactions are one place where learners can practice cultivating some of these knowledge-processing behaviors. However, as reference librarians know, it can be difficult to choose when to give learners quick answers and when to provide more in-depth assistance that pushes learners to evaluate information sources more critically or to recognize when to ask different questions to address a problem. Sometimes these decisions are made based on the practicality of time pressures and the many needs of learners waiting in line at the reference desk. And sometimes learners have to hear the same advice but from multiple people in different contexts in order to learn how to ask their own questions (see the Real-Life Reference Example). This section will examine how librarians can use reference interactions to help learners see ill-structured problems differently.

The Reflective Judgment Model provides several opportunities for working with learners on ill-structured or uncomfortable questions. A common question at the reference desk or via chat reference is for help selecting sources. At academic libraries, the emphasis is often on how to choose scholarly sources. Librarians have sometimes relied on simple mnemonics such as the CRAAP (Currency, Relevance, Authority, Accuracy, Purpose) test to efficiently guide learners through the process of evaluating sources (Blakeslee 2004). This checklist approach is meant to help learners easily navigate the process of choosing quality sources. However, a simplistic approach often ignores the context of both the information need and the purpose for which the source was created. For example, different sources will be appropriate for an assignment asking learners to present an explanatory speech about a current issue than for an assignment dealing with historical implications of an issue. In the same vein, a scholarly article on genetics research written twenty years ago

REAL-LIFE REFERENCE EXAMPLE

In a recent consult, I met with an undergraduate student who wanted to apply concepts she learned in her economics courses (her major) to a research paper for a sociology research methods course for which I had given a one-shot library session focused on search strategies and relevant resources. After some struggle researching on her own and after consulting with a sociology professor and an economics professor, the student reached out to me for help with locating sources. Even though the student had received specific library instruction, it wasn't until after she struggled with the messiness of research on her own that she realized the need to ask more nuanced questions and to engage more deeply. While discussing her topic, she realized she needed, and was empowered, to translate concepts between the two disciplines. She also learned she could use the name of a specific data set as a search term. Prompted by this spark for her learning, she wondered, "Why don't they teach this kind of research to everybody?" From my perspective, even though the research process was not straightforward and was frustrating, ultimately she developed her knowledge about both disciplines and the need to persevere on her path.

—Jane Nichols, Oregon State University,
personal communication, February 16, 2016

won't be a good source for a paper on current techniques, even if the paper was published in a prestigious journal. Ignoring the context of these sources and how they will be used leads to a poor understanding of the purpose of using scholarly evidence.

Because of the brief and ephemeral nature of many reference interactions—especially chat reference interactions—librarians don't always get the full contextual background for the information need. Due to the wide availability of many types of information sources, standards are now shifting to focus on a deeper understanding of the context in which authority is established (ACRL 2016; Seeber 2016). Here are two suggestions for promoting a richer understanding of context within reference consultations to help learners improve their ability to address hard questions.

The first suggestion is to be up front about the fluid nature of authority. Rather than presenting sources as good or bad, Leanne Bowler suggests moving toward the "greyer zone of better and best" (2010, 39). Encourage learners not to rely on surface-level context clues such as the domain of a web address (e.g., .edu, .org, .com) but instead to focus on the CRAAP authority checklist questions that require deeper questioning such as an exploration of the author's credentials and publishing history. For example, show learners an academic author's Google Scholar Citations page to demonstrate what topics the author typically writes on and the author's impact within their field. When looking at blogs or websites, discuss Google's author ranking process and how this process makes certain authors' works display more prominently. Modeling these types of questions with learners in a reference interaction can help create a more contextual view of authority that enables learners to ask questions on their own when faced with new decisions about information.

The second suggestion is to verbalize ill-structured problems that you face in your own work as a librarian. Issues such as open access or copyright are not cut and dried and require asking many questions repeatedly and engaging with people who hold a variety of perspectives. When starting a search on the library's website, note the pros and cons of searching within an environment that includes subscription-based content, and discuss why your library chooses to subscribe to the content it does. Include Google or other broad search engines in your reference repertoire, and mention how you are determining what content is authoritative or what content might be appropriate to reuse. Bowler (2010) argues that showing learners that uncertainty exists in the information-seeking process can help learners feel less anxious and normalizes the iterative process of creating new knowledge.

In summary, some reference strategies that are appropriate for encouraging learners to ask deeper questions include

- demonstrating that authority changes based on the context and
- modeling how you deal with hard questions.

Reference interactions come in many forms including quick questions at a reference desk, questions received via an e-mail or chat box, and in-depth research consultations. Naturally, your opportunities to engage learners in more context-dependent ways of asking questions will vary depending on the form of the reference interaction, but start small with at least one of these suggestions to discover ways to make this practice work for you.

Library Instruction and the Reflective Judgment Model

Instruction sessions provide librarians with more time and the ability to structure in-class activities that allow learners to develop their questioning abilities. Unlike at a reference desk, in an instruction session, librarians don't need to wait for learners to come to them with questions but instead get to shape a shared experience that emphasizes ill-structured questions. Librarians' ownership over the content covered is strongest in a credit-based course or in workshops they design. Librarians have somewhat less control over the content when delivering one-shot sessions in support of an assignment created by disciplinary instructors or faculty. However, creating partnerships allows librarians to offer an alternative solution to problems faculty members may be experiencing in their classrooms and to advocate for different approaches to creating assignments or for conceptualizing learners' role in the research process. (See the Real-Life Instruction Solution for one approach to a common instruction problem.) This section will look at how instruction librarians can highlight ill-structured questions in the research process to help learners consider new ways of looking at the world around them.

REAL-LIFE INSTRUCTION SOLUTION

I had a student who was convinced that aliens built the pyramids and refused to accept the literature that conflicted with this belief. One of the things the librarians here have started to cover in the IL [information literacy] sessions (especially if it's for some kind of speech/debate class) is that sometimes research may conflict with your personal beliefs. We emphasize that just because the students make an argument in a paper, they don't have to necessarily agree with it in their personal life.
—Hillary Fox, University of West Florida, STS-L listserv, February 17, 2016

As discussed in chapter 2, as learners develop intellectually, they are increasingly able to deal with ambiguity. The one-shot exercises provided in chapter 2 suggested encouraging learners to explore and use different source types depending on their intellectual development stage. Using the lens of the Reflective Judgment Model, another way to encourage learners to grow in their understanding of how to use appropriate sources for different contexts is to focus on how the knowledge in those sources is constructed. This section will give examples of some ill-structured questions about knowledge creation that librarians could address in the classroom.

In academic libraries, the conversation around quality sources or source evaluation often centers on defining what scholarly, peer-reviewed literature looks like and how to find this type of literature. However, the questions of "what is peer-reviewed literature" and "why should I use peer-reviewed literature" are actually ill-structured questions that provide excellent opportunities for instruction librarians to encourage learners to reflect on different ways to reframe these questions.

One classroom exercise to help highlight the complexity of "what is peer-reviewed literature" is to start by assigning learners three to five serials that use a variety of kinds of review (e.g., editorial review, blind peer review, or open peer review) and then ask the class to look those serials up in a database such as Ulrichsweb. Ask learners to record whether or not Ulrichsweb categorizes these serials as being refereed or not. Then ask learners to go to each serial's website to see how the serial describes itself and what range of articles it publishes. It is likely that learners will find inconsistencies between the information provided by Ulrichsweb and the information from the serials' website. For example, the *Journal of Forestry* is classified as a refereed journal in Ulrichsweb but is actually more of a hybrid trade publication/scholarly journal that serves professional foresters by providing research articles as well as personal reflections, book reviews, discussions about hot topics, and a forestry quiz. Looking at specific serials might make easy categorization more difficult but can lead to a discussion about how the interplay between audience and author results in varied ways of contextualizing information.

If you are conducting a session in partnership with a disciplinary faculty member, choose serials from that faculty member's discipline, and ask the faculty member to discuss how they would rank and evaluate those serials. Again, encourage learners to reflect on how the designation of "refereed" or "peer reviewed" may not be as cut and dried as they may have initially thought (or been taught). Because serials often publish a wide range of articles, from peer-reviewed articles to editorials and book reviews, it can be difficult to make sweeping statements about whether or not an entire serial is peer reviewed. In addition, asking the faculty member to talk through how they think about serials will reveal a new set of questions to ask about how to select serials for different purposes such as, does the prestige of this serial matter, is the serial open access, or do practitioners read it?

Another classroom exercise can examine the question of "why should I use peer-reviewed literature" by exploring how scholars use peer-reviewed literature. Divide learners into pairs, and give them excerpts from the literature review and the discussion sections of a scholarly article relevant to their class or discipline. These two sections of an article are useful for this exercise because they both incorporate information from outside sources. Give the class highlighters, and ask them to identify places in the literature review where the authors are building on the work of others to develop their own research question. Learners could look for examples of comparisons, contrasts, or historical background. Then ask learners to identify what questions or ideas for future research the authors identify in the discussion or conclusion sections.

Walking through this type of exercise can help demonstrate that the role of peer-reviewed literature is not meant to be a simple workaround for quickly identifying quality sources but is intended to build up a conversation within a particular discipline where authors rely on past research to help develop new questions (Deitering and Gronemyer 2011). Scholars are not searching for an answer but rather are trying to build up questions to study (Exner 2014). Once you have illustrated the ways that scholars ask questions, finish this exercise by asking each of the pairs to come up with their own follow-up questions about either their own topics or a topic the class is working on jointly.

Another classroom context in which to model iterative question-asking behaviors is in workshops for graduate students. Many academic libraries offer literature review workshops. New graduate students often struggle with the burden of determining whether or not they are exploring a unique or worthwhile question in their thesis, while at the same time they need to build on previous scholarship. As a result, graduate students often choose a scope for their project that is too narrow and end up concluding there isn't any appropriate background information on their topic (Bruce 2001). To provide graduate students with a strategy for developing questions that equips them with better ways to approach previous scholarship, walk through the iterative question-based approach to the literature review schematic with your class (see figure 3.2).

An Iterative Question-Based Approach to the Literature Review Process

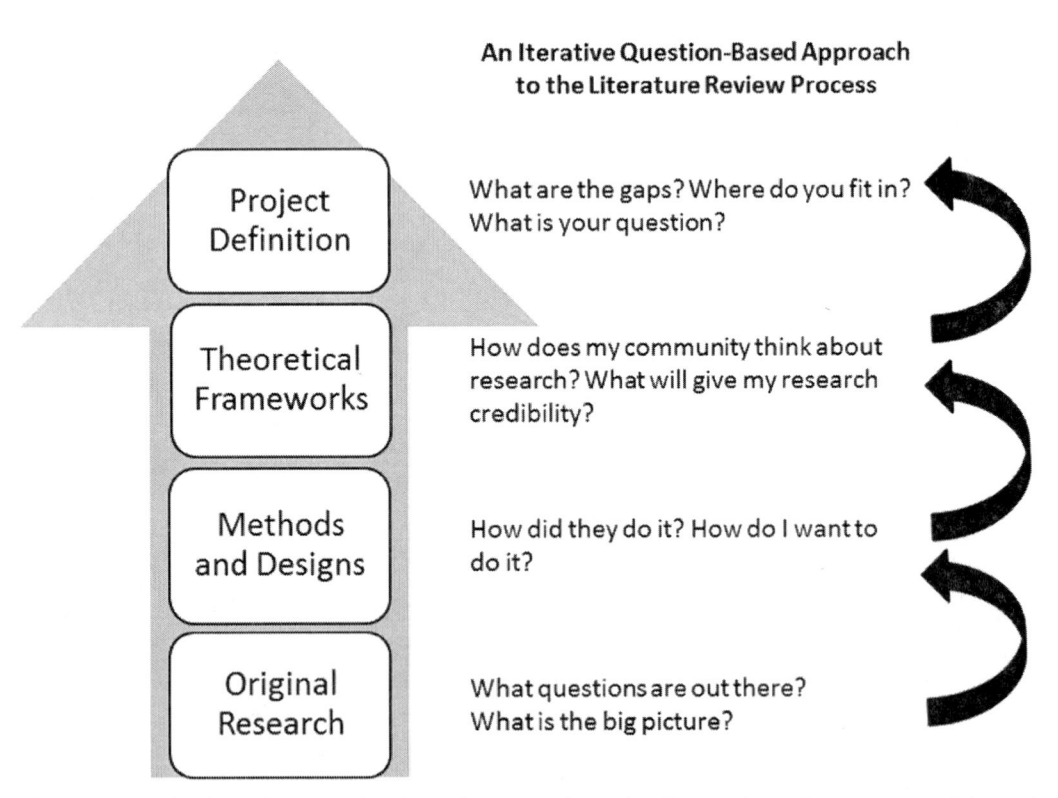

- **Project Definition** — What are the gaps? Where do you fit in? What is your question?
- **Theoretical Frameworks** — How does my community think about research? What will give my research credibility?
- **Methods and Designs** — How did they do it? How do I want to do it?
- **Original Research** — What questions are out there? What is the big picture?

Figure 3.2. An iterative question-based approach to the literature review process. *Adapted from Exner 2014.*

This schematic outlines an iterative question-asking approach that should take place throughout the literature review process. Encourage learners to start by looking broadly at the original research in a particular field and reading to find out what types of questions researchers are asking. Next, graduate students can look at the methods and designs in the literature and ask, how is this kind of research done? Once the practical considerations of how the research might be conducted are in place, students can reread the literature to ask, what techniques does my research community use to signal credibility or professionalism? For example, do they traditionally use models, particular statistics, or certain types of graphs? Finally, after establishing a broader sense of what the background literature reports, graduate students can ask, where are the gaps in the literature, and what is my question?

Instruction librarians have a great opportunity to model and illustrate the complexity of the research process. Some of these exercises are more appropriate for advanced learners such as graduate students. But being willing to admit when you don't know the answer, and then working together with your learners to find either an answer or more questions, can empower a wide range of learners to feel more confident in asking their own questions. In summary, some instructional strategies that give learners a chance to explore ill-structured questions include

- exploring how scholars themselves use information to develop more questions and
- modeling ways to ask different questions at different stages of the research process.

Library Outreach and the Reflective Judgment Model

As noted in chapter 2, library outreach activities provide opportunities for more creative and nontraditional ways to engage learners around information problems, sticky questions, reflection, and information-creation possibilities. Library outreach activities take place in all types of libraries, and the following examples could be applied in a range of settings. Based on the findings from the Project Information Literacy study of young adults, opportunities for growth and more engagement with this particular population (and arguably, other adult populations) may be increasingly valuable (Head 2016). Just a note, many excellent outreach activities for children and youth are well established at public libraries, but those will not be covered in this section.

Keeping the adult, and particularly the young adult, demographic in mind when thinking about how to incorporate intellectual development theories can provide context for new outreach activities you develop. While intellectual development strategies might not always be used explicitly in outreach activities, based on your understanding of the foundational principles of the Reflective Judgment Model, you will likely see opportunities for encouraging question asking in many outreach scenarios. This section will examine how outreach librarians can bring together a community of learners to engage in tough questions from a range of perspectives.

Learners representing a wide range of ages and educational backgrounds are increasingly becoming involved in citizen science efforts. Citizen science draws on open science principles and encourages addressing tough scientific questions by collaboratively collecting data and openly sharing the resulting research data. One of the main goals of projects such as these is to create spaces where people can reuse the data in new ways to solve problems the original researchers may not even have considered. Libraries can serve both as venues for hosting groups that work on citizen science efforts and as facilitators for considering some of the complexities behind dealing with open data.

One example of a library that has offered citizen science outreach events is the Hennepin County Library's annual Geo:Code event. At this daylong event, participants create new maps using freely available data (http://www.hennepin.us/geocode). This event is targeted at both experts and novices who are interested in using maps to display information such as bicycle facilities, road construction and road closures, and free fresh food access. Volunteers help to generate the ideas, and the practical nature of many of these projects makes the work appealing to a wide audience.

However, one of the issues that emerges with open data is that the data is often messy: it may be improperly labeled, not labeled at all, or available in a format that is no longer useful. While issues around data curation and the importance of metadata are familiar for many librarians, community members may not have considered how to deal with these complex questions before. At an outreach event focused on citizen science activities, librarians should consider including some time for reflection and discussion around the issues of dealing with messy data. Facilitating these types of conversations can prompt learners to think not only of research data in new ways but also about their own personal data-management practices in a new light.

Key Points

Understanding ways that you can both challenge and support your learners as they encounter increasingly complicated problems can help you provide library services that are relevant for the shifting needs of your learner population. Here are some key points to take away:

- Some problems don't have clear-cut answers and need to be revisited from multiple angles to more fully understand them.
- Library activities that encourage and model deeper question-asking can help learners practice dealing with these kinds of ill-structured problems.

The Reflective Judgment Model provides fodder for thinking about strategies for encouraging your learners to tackle difficult questions. Another major consideration in intellectual development is the recognition that individual backgrounds and experiences have a large impact on learners' approach to asking questions and solving problems. Chapter 4 will guide you through another intellectual development theory that recognizes the importance of these different experiences and will discuss ways to incorporate that theory into your work as a librarian.

References

ACRL (Association of College and Research Libraries). 2016. "Framework for Information Literacy for Higher Education." January 11. http://www.ala.org/.

ALA (American Library Association) Council. 2004. "Core Values of Librarianship." ALA, June 29. http://www.ala.org/.

———. 2016. "Framework for Information Literacy for Higher Education." ALA, January 11. http://www.ala.org/.

Blakeslee, Sarah. 2004. "The CRAAP Test." *LOEX Quarterly* 31 (3): 6–7.

Bowler, Leanne. 2010. "A Taxonomy of Adolescent Metacognitive Knowledge during the Information Search Process." *Library and Information Science Research* 32 (1): 27–42. doi:10.1016/j.lisr.2009.09.005.

Bruce, Christine S. 2001. "Interpreting the Scope of Their Literature Reviews: Significant Differences in Research Students' Concerns." *New Library World* 102:158–65.

Chatman, Elfreda A. 1999. "A Theory of Life in the Round." *Journal of the Association for Information Science and Technology* 50 (3): 207–17.

Deitering, Anne-Marie, and Kate Gronemyer. 2011. "Beyond Peer-Reviewed Articles: Using Blogs to Enrich Students' Understanding of Scholarly Work." *portal: Libraries and the Academy* 11 (1): 489–503.

Exner, Nina. 2014. "Research Information Literacy: Addressing Original Researchers' Needs." *Journal of Academic Librarianship* 40 (5): 460–66. doi:10.1016/j.acalib.2014.06.006.

Head, Alison J. 2016. "Staying Smart: How Today's Graduates Continue to Learn Once They Complete College." Project Information Literacy Research Report, University of Washington, Seattle, January 5. http://papers.ssrn.com/.

King, Patricia M., and Karen S. Kitchener. 1994. *Developing Reflective Judgment: Understanding and Promoting Intellectual Growth and Critical Thinking in Adolescents and Adults.* San Francisco: Jossey-Bass.

Mirani, Leo. 2014. "Turns Out Twitter Is Even More Politically Polarized than You Thought." Quartz, February 20. http://qz.com/.

Pariser, Eli. 2011. "Beware Online 'Filter Bubbles.'" TED Talk. http://www.ted.com/.

Rempel, Hannah Gascho, Stefanie Buck, and Anne-Marie Deitering. 2013. "Examining Student Research Choices and Processes in a Disintermediated Searching Environment." *portal: Libraries and the Academy* 13 (4): 363–84.

Seeber, Kevin. 2016. "It's Not a Competition! Questioning the Rhetoric of 'Scholarly versus Popular' in Library Instruction." Presented at the Critical Librarianship and Pedagogy Symposium, Tucson, Arizona, February 25. http://kevinseeber.com/CLAPS2016.pdf.

CHAPTER 4

Building on Past Learning Experiences

IN THIS CHAPTER

▷ Understanding how different life experiences impact intellectual development
▷ Using reflection as a means for understanding contextual cues

---

IN YOUR WORK WITH LEARNERS, YOU have likely observed learners struggling to figure out how to align their past experiences with new information they find throughout the research process. The last chapter introduced the Reflective Judgment Model as a way to understand how learners approach increasingly complex and sticky problems. While learners' ability to deal with these complex problems does progress through developmental stages, without directed practice many learners may not have sufficient strategies for asking questions that will help them solve these problems. Chapter 3 presented some activities and modeling opportunities that librarians can use to help encourage learners to develop their abilities to ask questions in different ways.

The theory discussed in this chapter—the Epistemological Reflection Model—recognizes that learners come from many different backgrounds and that these different background experiences influence the intellectual strategies learners use. Feeling confident in expressing opinions that are different from the mainstream, engaging with a range of new ways of thinking, and maintaining a sense of one's own internal perspective are all intellectual abilities that mature and develop over time. The Epistemological Reflection Model suggests that effectively valuing the different experiences learners bring involves creating a culture of reflection. Within the space created through reflection, learners can be empowered to draw on their past contexts to interpret and apply new information.

Because the students studied in Perry's Intellectual and Ethical Development Theory were so homogenous, this chapter will look at research exploring how intellectual development theories can be more broadly applied to populations with diverse ages, genders, races, or socioeconomic statuses. Again, instead of focusing on specific developmental stages in this model, the examples provided will focus on the key principles from the Epistemological Reflection Model and how librarians can apply those principles within the contexts of reference, instruction, and outreach. This chapter will provide practical strategies and activities librarians can use with learners to encourage deeper, reflective thinking that incorporates different background experiences.

Cognitive-Structural Theories in New Contexts

Chapter 2 introduced cognitive-structural theories—the group of theories that describe how people think, reason, and make decisions. The first theory discussed, William Perry's Intellectual and Ethical Development Theory, was based on white, middle-class, predominantly male, traditional, college-aged student behaviors. This chapter will continue to use examples from that age group but will also incorporate strategies from a theory that addresses intellectual development challenges that extend later into life and that takes into account a more diverse range of experiences.

While some librarians may interact with a well-defined, homogenous group of learners, many work with learners who arrive at their library with a wide range of past educational and cultural experiences and expectations about how knowledge is created and used. Public librarians have a large role in engaging with learners once they leave school, but school and academic librarians also frequently encounter learners with a variety of life experiences, including K–12 students transferring from other locations, nontraditional undergraduates, learners seeking postbaccalaureate or certificate training, and graduate students (see the Real-Life Librarian Experience). Librarians may not be experts in each of the areas or experiences represented by these learners, but the guidance provided by cognitive-structural theories can help create a framework for working with diverse learners.

> **REAL-LIFE LIBRARIAN EXPERIENCE**
>
> I work in a bilingual (Spanish) University, and I am monolingual, so nearly every workday I have this experience. I don't know if the English [language] learners understand or if they are just nodding their head. They are busy with jobs and families and make the giant leap to add college into the mix, and when they attend our university they must contend with textbooks written in English and additionally some faculty, like myself, who don't speak Spanish. Luckily online translators help the students and me to get our points across more or less, although translation is tricky. Ideas don't always translate directly between Spanish and English. As a result, from teaching my library orientations to new students to one-on-one tutoring sessions, this is a regular experience/problem.
> —Anonymous librarian, personal communication, February 4, 2016

Many of the principles of intellectual development hold true for a wide spectrum of learners, but observing where differences arise based on gender, cultural background, and socioeconomic status can help librarians articulate the need for a variety of approaches for developing learners' problem-solving capabilities through a range of library services.

The next sections will provide background information for the Epistemological Reflection Model so that librarians will be able to create services that reflect the needs of an increasingly diverse population.

Epistemological Reflection Model

Patricia King and Karen Kitchener expanded on earlier theories in their Reflective Judgment Model by exploring how learners approach difficult questions across a much broader age range. However, like Perry, their studies were based primarily on middle-class white people from the upper Midwest and as a result cannot necessarily be applied to people beyond this homogenous group. While they did do some analysis of their model by gender, this type of differentiation was not the primary intention of their work. Educational researcher Marcia Baxter Magolda sought to remedy that gap and developed the Epistemological Reflection Model in part to describe differences in the way people understand and use knowledge. Her research specifically addressed gender, but other researchers have built on the Epistemological Reflection Model to understand a range of diverse contexts including race and socioeconomic status (Howard-Hamilton 2003; Torres and Baxter Magolda 2004).

Baxter Magolda developed her model based on interviews with 101 first-year students at Miami University, a midsize public university in Ohio. Half of the participants were female, and half were male, but only three students were from racially nondominant populations (Baxter Magolda 1992). She repeated her interviews with these same students once each year over the course of five years—including the year immediately following graduation. Amazingly, seventy participants persisted through all five interviews.

The Epistemological Reflection Model contains what Baxter Magolda terms "four ways of knowing" (1992, 29):

- Absolute knowing
- Transitional knowing
- Independent knowing
- Contextual knowing

Again, similar to the Intellectual and Ethical Development Theory and the Reflective Judgment Model, the first stage describes a way of knowing that views knowledge as absolute and then progresses through ways of knowing that acknowledge some uncertainty, and eventually understandings of knowledge develop to a point where more context and relevant evidence are considered. Baxter Magolda found that traditional college-aged students typically progressed through at least the first two stages during college, but students rarely reached the third or fourth stages until after college.

Women have historically been understudied in psychology (and other fields), and so Baxter Magolda chose to explore what differences might exist in her model between women and men. She found trends, which she calls "reasoning patterns" (1992, 193), demonstrating several differences as women and men progress through the four stages of knowing (see table 4.1). While these three reasoning patterns change as people transition to other stages of knowing, overall women tend to receive and interact with knowledge outside of the classroom in a more private sphere, they bounce their ideas off of other people, and they gather input from people they trust. Women do not tend to rely on

Table 4.1. Epistemological Reflection Model gender patterns

	PERCEPTION OF KNOWLEDGE	WOMEN	MEN
Absolute knowing	Knowledge is certain or absolute.	Receive knowledge: interact with authorities only when they need clarification, usually outside of class	Master knowledge: trying to learn to become authorities, participate in practicing what they know in class
Transitional knowing	Some knowledge is uncertain.	Recognize individual and interpersonal differences	Impersonal knowing focused on logic, debate, and research
Independent knowing	Knowledge is mostly uncertain.	Value inter-individual exchanges: sharing their own opinions and hearing others' opinions	Value reasoning on their own to arrive at opinions and ideas
Contextual knowing	Knowledge is contextual, and evidence needs to be evaluated.	No clear gender patterns	

Source: Adapted from Baxter Magolda 1992 and Evans et al. 2010.

instructors as models for learning unless they have a high degree of trust in them. In addition, women tend to see knowledge as containing elements of uncertainty sooner than men do. Men tend to try out their new ideas more publicly, for example, in a classroom setting; they value knowledge that is presented logically; and they increasingly rely on their own expertise. Interestingly, gender-based differences disappeared by the fourth stage—contextual knowing (Baxter Magolda 1992; Evans et al. 2010). See the Advanced Learners One-Shot Library Instruction Scenario—Revisited for an example where a librarian observes intellectual development differences based on gender.

ADVANCED LEARNERS ONE-SHOT LIBRARY INSTRUCTION SCENARIO—REVISITED

To better understand the impact of gender on intellectual approaches, picture yourself as the librarian in the following scenario. Ask yourself how different "reasoning patterns" could help you explain students' behavior in these classes.

Earlier you led a nutrition class through a problem-based exercise based on a real-life case study. Later that week, you lead an exercise and sport science class through a very similar exercise. However, unlike the nutrition sciences class, which was made up entirely of women, the exercise and sport science class was much more balanced in terms of gender. You observe that when the students are working in groups, the women are more likely to start the conversation by soliciting the opinions of others in the group, while the men are more likely to start by offering their own opinions.

Not all of these students fall into neat categories, but the gendered behaviors observed in the exercise and sport sciences class match Baxter Magolda's independent knowing stage in the Epistemological Reflection Model in terms of the ways men and women sometimes seek to explore new information.

Baxter Magolda is quick to note that gender-based differences are highly context dependent and that obviously not all men will act in one way and all women in another way. Many people exhibit characteristics that overlap into reasoning patterns based not on gender but on other factors such as their race, ethnicity, or socioeconomic class. Much of the value of Baxter Magolda's research is the emphasis she places on understanding context. For example, she points out that women's ways of behaving are shaped by a variety of factors, including centuries of societal expectations that funneled them into certain job types and household roles. As a result, it is not surprising that some women would shy away from exploring new ideas or ways of knowing in more public venues. Similarly, African Americans have been consistently discriminated against and socialized to internalize that their lives have less value than the dominant culture; therefore, Baxter Magolda observes that many African Americans have learned to set up protective mechanisms and may not assert their authority or knowledge within larger, mixed-race groups. In addition, traditionally marginalized people can approach information seeking differently. People from privileged backgrounds may need encouragement to step outside of the filter bubbles or closed social networks that make it difficult to engage with other perspectives (Pariser 2011). In contrast, librarian activist nina de jesus argues that historically marginalized peoples are continually exposed to worldviews or knowledge with which they are uncomfortable. Rather than needing to seek out diverse views, de jesus notes how important it is for traditionally marginalized peoples to find online information sources and communities that validate their voices (de jesus 2014).

The importance of context is also important within educational systems. Baxter Magolda hypothesizes that perhaps the reason students don't progress further through the four ways of knowing during college is that higher education continues to emphasize hierarchical power structures with clear authority roles. Under this framework, professors are the ones who give authoritative information, and it is the student's role to receive that information. As a result, students continue to rely on outside authorities rather than learning to develop their own understanding of how information and knowledge are created.

The Epistemological Reflection Model offers three main recommendations for changing the higher education setting and informing instructional practices. First, learners must be given opportunities to develop their own voices and ask complex questions so their value as a "knower" is clear. Second, learners' personal experiences should be recognized and validated within instructional settings. Finally, learners and instructors (or librarians) need to work together to explore knowledge and be responsible for constructing meaning. These recommendations overlap and build on the recommendations described in chapter 2, which included providing safe spaces, giving clear directions, and introducing alternative viewpoints within reference, instruction, and outreach settings. A variety of strategies for incorporating these recommendations into librarians' practice will be discussed later in this chapter.

EPISTEMOLOGICAL REFLECTION MODEL
TRANSFORMATIVE EDUCATIONAL PRACTICES

- Give learners opportunities to develop their own voice.
- Recognize and value learners' personal experiences.
- Instructors and learners explore and learn together.

Because of the lack of diversity in her study sample, Baxter Magolda acknowledged that the transferability of her findings may be somewhat limited. However, her emphasis on listening to learners within their own unique context is a valuable exercise, and the Epistemological Reflection Model provides additional ways for categorizing and thinking about how your learners can experience knowledge based on a variety of contextual factors. Each learner's individual context is a major factor in shaping his or her reactions to authority, evidence, and making meaning, so considering these factors can help provide new insights as you create learning experiences that best match your learners' developmental stages.

Increasingly, librarians are embracing the challenge to move beyond the mechanics of showing learners how to find information to providing opportunities for interacting more directly with information. The next section will discuss ways that librarians can use the Epistemological Reflection Model to create safe, affirming spaces where learners can develop their own abilities to reflect, ask questions, and practice using a wide range of information sources in a variety of contexts.

Applying the Epistemological Reflection Model to the Library Context

The Epistemological Reflection Model's key principle is providing opportunities for structured reflection within a variety of contexts. Librarians have some distinct advantages because they already work with learners in a range of contexts. Librarians meet with learners online, in neutral meeting spaces, in offices, in public spaces, and in the classroom. In addition, librarians' relationship with learners is usually less formal than learners' relationship with teachers or government officials. While some librarians teach for-credit classes, the majority of librarian-learner interactions take place outside of the traditional instructor-student power dynamic (although a certain level of perceived authority likely still remains). Working outside of this power dynamic allows librarians to interact with learners in a potentially more transformational way. As Baxter Magolda noted, "Learning is a relational activity and education is often not relational" (Evans et al. 2010, 129). Approaching interactions with learners in a relational way makes it easier for librarians to explore new ideas and create knowledge together within a range of library settings.

Reference Consultations and the Epistemological Reflection Model

The Epistemological Reflection Model encourages learners to use reflective thinking as a way to solve problems. One way to encourage more reflective thinking in reference interactions is to use a tutoring-based approach. A tutor works together with a learner to solve problems, rather than giving learners a lengthy lecture or a simplistic solution (Eckel 2007). Educational researchers who study tutoring best practices have found that tutors use a variety of techniques to prompt learners to reflect on questions and problems and to become an active part of the learning process (Person and Graesser 1999). Five of these tutoring techniques can be translated particularly well to reference interactions: splicing, prompting, hinting, pumping, and summarizing (see table 4.2).

Using these tutoring techniques isn't like following a recipe—you don't have to start with the first technique and continue through to the last technique. A sampling of these techniques can be used throughout reference interactions to encourage learners to reflect

Table 4.2. Tutoring techniques that encourage shared problem solving

TECHNIQUE	DEFINITION	LEVEL OF COGNITIVE EFFORT FOR THE STUDENT
Splicing	Librarian and learner work together to complete thoughts; librarian interrupts to splice in a corrected or new idea.	Low
Prompting	The librarian starts a phrase, and the learner completes the rest of the idea.	Low
Hinting	The librarian directs learners away from misconceptions by prompting the learner in the right direction.	Low–medium
Pumping	Verbal (e.g., affirmation) and nonverbal (e.g., nodding) cues are used to encourage the learner to keep going and expand on ideas.	Medium
Summarizing	The learners are encouraged to summarize how they have solved their problem and what they have learned.	High

Source: Adapted from Person and Graesser 1999.

on their problem-solving process rather than waiting for someone else to provide all the answers. That said, consider ending a reference interaction by encouraging learners to try out more cognitively demanding techniques such as summarizing to help learners solve problems on their own more effectively.

Person and Graesser refer to an overall strategy of "modeling-scaffolding-fading" in which the tutor (or in this case, the librarian) initially contributes more of the cognitive energy by modeling how they answer a question (1999, 80). Next, the librarian gives the learner practice walking through a guided or scaffolded problem-solving process in partnership with the librarian. Finally, the librarian fades into the background so the learner can solve problems on their own based on reflective thinking practices they have tried with the librarian. See the Tutoring Techniques in a Sample Reference Interaction scenario for an example of how the five tutoring techniques might be applied in a reference consultation with an undergraduate student.

TUTORING TECHNIQUES IN A SAMPLE REFERENCE INTERACTION

- Starting topic: Concussions in sports
- Ending topic: What implications does gender have on the prevalence of concussions in precollegiate and collegiate sports?

Splicing

LEARNER: I want to explore concussions in sports, and I played girls' soccer in high school, so I wondered if there was a connection there. I looked for some sources using the library's search tools, but I couldn't find anything.

LIBRARIAN: You looked in the library's 1Search [discovery] tool?

LEARNER: Yeah, that's the one. And I have to find unbiased research articles, but I couldn't figure out how to do that.

LIBRARIAN: You needed peer-reviewed research articles?
LEARNER: Yes, that's what my professor called them.
LIBRARIAN: Okay, let's start by looking in 1Search together and then we can consider some other options from there.

Prompting
LIBRARIAN: What keywords did you try entering earlier?
LEARNER: Concussion, girls soccer, and high school
LIBRARIAN: What kinds of articles were you hoping to find?
LEARNER: I don't know, research articles but with a general overview, some good background.

Hinting
LIBRARIAN: So what might be some other words for girls, maybe some broader terms?
LEARNER: Females, women
LIBRARIAN: What if you wanted to compare results for men and women athletes? What terms do you think a scientist might use?
LEARNER: Male and female, oh, and I've also had a gender studies class. So maybe gender?

Pumping
LIBRARIAN: Look at the results list we have now. What do you notice?
LEARNER: Well, I really want articles on soccer, but all these other sports keep coming up.
LIBRARIAN: Good observation—so you're reading the titles and don't see soccer listed?
LEARNER: Yeah, and I tried gender instead of girls and I keep having the same problem.
LIBRARIAN: Have you looked at the abstracts or any other information?
LEARNER: No. How do I do that?
LIBRARIAN: Let's open some of these abstracts and articles together to see how we can scan for more details.

Summarizing
LIBRARIAN: So we started with a question based on your high school experiences; where did we end up?
LEARNER: Well, I made my keywords a little broader and more scientific sounding.
LIBRARIAN: When you read through some of these articles on your own, what can you look for?
LEARNER: I'll definitely look more at the abstracts, and then maybe at some of the data or tables to see if there is information that I want to pull out.

Just like tutors, librarians work with learners who have a wide range of past experiences with asking questions, researching, and libraries in general. Using these tutoring techniques is a way to meet learners where they are and then to give them a framework for thinking through questions on their own. The five tutoring techniques are also referred to as "conversational moves" (Person and Graesser 1999, 80). Thinking of reference interactions as conversations, to which both librarians and learners contribute, helps learners take ownership for their own learning. In summary, some reference strategies that will encourage learners to reflect on their own learning include

- starting with easier prompts and ending with time for self-reflection and summary
- working together with learners to solve problems

Library Instruction and the Epistemological Reflection Model

Library instruction sessions provide many opportunities for learners to practice their reflecting abilities so they can consider new ways of looking at the world around them. Providing learners with the space and capacity for reflecting on their own learning is a powerful way to work with learners to develop critical questioning skills. Encouraging learners to use reflective thinking to solve problems is at the heart of the Epistemological Reflection Model. Some learners turn to reflection more naturally than others, and most people are easily distracted by the demands of outside life. As a result, creating intentional opportunities for reflection within instructional settings is crucial for developing learners' reflection habits. Modeling multiple ways of reflecting can help learners build up a range of approaches to choose from that work best for them. This section will describe several reflective exercises that can be used in library instruction sessions.

The first exercise is an assumption audit (James and Brookfield 2014). Each learner begins the research process with some previous knowledge and assumptions about a topic, but it can be easy to ignore these starting assumptions. One way to introduce this concept is to explicitly talk through some of your own assumptions about a topic and what informs your thinking. Another technique is to provide several written prompts for learners to reflect on and then respond to (see the Assumption Audit Reflection Prompts box below). Assumptions about a topic may be quite personal, so using this as an ungraded, in-class activity will likely work best. If you have the opportunity to interact with a class multiple times, ask the class to revisit their assumptions about a topic to see if or how their thoughts and feelings have shifted over time.

ASSUMPTION AUDIT REFLECTION PROMPTS

- What do you know about this topic?
- What do you feel about this topic?
- Where have you heard other people express the same knowledge or feelings?
- Where have you heard other people express alternative knowledge or feelings?

Some reflection is best done privately, but some learners reflect better through talking than through writing. Use pair-share activities to provide the opportunity for learners to reflect on an assigned prompt. One way to encourage learners to view a topic from multiple viewpoints is to assign each pair a controversial topic that is relevant to the course material. Depending on how much previous exposure learners may have had to the issue, provide a short written summary of the topic and some of the potential sides or arguments that already exist on this topic. Ask one learner to find two sources for one side of the issue and the other learner to find two sources for an alternative side of the issue. The sources can be scholarly if that is important for the course, but they do not need to be. After the learners have found sources to support their issue, ask them to summarize the key points from the two sources for their partner. Give learners a handout with note-taking prompts to capture the information their partners identify (see table 4.3). Next, to encourage learners to better understand how someone else thinks, ask the learners to swap sides. Based on the source summary information their partners provided, ask the learners to engage in a brief debate about this topic and to try to arrive at a consensus. Make it clear that the goal of this debate is not to determine a winner or to find a perfect solution to the issue; rather, it is to encourage learners to experience an alternative point of view. Finish this exercise by reflecting as a group about how it felt to argue from a different viewpoint after investing time and effort in an alternative point of view.

Another reflection activity that can be done in pairs introduces the value of exploring knowledge from other fields outside of your learners' initial area of interest. This activity is best done after learners have chosen their topics and done exploratory research. Randomly assign learners to pairs, or if you know what topic each person has chosen, intentionally pair learners with someone who is exploring a topic that is quite different from their own. Next, ask learners to find common points of overlap between their two topics. Initially, this might be difficult, but encourage learners to either keep taking one step backward until they can find a point of commonality or to think about their topic from a completely new angle. For example, one learner might be researching the Greek life system, and another learner may be exploring the legalization of marijuana. Some potential points of overlap could include exploring how social norms are established, or looking at how the actions of a few individuals influence the rules or laws that are put in place for larger groups. The value of this exercise is that it encourages learners to work together to challenge their initial assumptions about a topic, to see their topic from a new vantage point, and to ask different questions than they may have started with.

Reflection is a valuable tool; however, it takes trust for learners to be able to share their reflections. As Alison James and Stephen Brookfield (2014) note, be careful not to ask learners to overreflect. Intersperse times of reflection with other learning activities and include both personal and group reflection times to build on different learners' communication strengths. Model these reflective behaviors by verbalizing what your own assumptions are and how your thinking about certain issues has changed over time. Not all reflection needs to result in big ideas or ground-breaking new questions.

Table 4.3. Multiple viewpoints note-taking guide

	SOURCE 1 SUMMARY (INCLUDE CITATION INFORMATION):	SOURCE 2 SUMMARY (INCLUDE CITATION INFORMATION):
Position 1	Main argument: Supporting data:	Main argument: Supporting data:
Position 2	Main argument: Supporting data:	Main argument: Supporting data:

Instead, the ability to reflect, even in small ways, throughout the learning process develops learners who are open to seeking new questions and perspectives. In summary, some instructional strategies that give learners a chance to reflect on their own learning include the following:

- Prompting learners to examine their underlying assumptions
- Approaching a problem from multiple vantage points
- Using a range of private and public, and written and spoken, reflection techniques
- Modeling your own habits of reflection

Library Outreach and the Epistemological Reflection Model

Because library outreach often involves programs or hands-on experiences, it may seem that reflective activities are out of place in library outreach programs. However, activities that push learners to see the world through someone else's viewpoint can encourage meaningful reflection, even if that reflection does not take the form of assigned journaling or responses to specific discussion prompts. Public libraries are already respected as gathering spaces with trusted experts on hand; as a result, they are well situated to provide outreach activities to a range of adults who may be new to a community, who are seeking to reinvent themselves in their community, or who simply want to continue growing as a lifelong learner. These growth opportunities require intentional reflection and a consideration of how one's past experiences might influence new interactions.

One example of an outreach activity that encourages growth is a Human Library event. Several libraries have hosted Human Library events to encourage connections between people with different backgrounds and life experiences. According to the Human Library Organization (http://humanlibrary.org/), the goal of these events is to help break down stereotypes and prejudices through one-on-one conversations. Patrons can check out a volunteer "book," that is, a person with a particular story to tell, and have a conversation with that person about those experiences. At Oregon State University Libraries, books included a person with experience being married to an undocumented immigrant, a military veteran, and an American immigrant from a Muslim country (Oregon State University 2016). Syracuse University has hosted three Human Library events where books could be "borrowed" for up to twenty-minute discussions. Topics included a person living with mental-health issues, a student who grew up on an Indian reservation, and a biracial trans individual (Syracuse University 2016). And at Geneva Public Library, books included a homeless person, a former butler, and a father of a heroin addict (Tulis 2015). A key component of these events is that all of the people who sign up as books do so voluntarily and not out of pressure to represent a traditionally marginalized group. Book topics can be thought of very broadly, especially if the focus is on including a variety of life experiences.

While speaking with someone with very different experiences can feel risky and may be uncomfortable at times, providing spaces for these unique interactions can encourage people to consider viewpoints outside of their normal filter bubble. Explicit reflection prompts may not be needed for a Human Library activity, but providing some quiet spaces or blank pieces of paper for participants to write on after their conversations can facilitate reflection opportunities for those who wish to process what they have heard in an intentional way.

Key Points

Learners come from a wide range of backgrounds and have different past experiences that inform how they face intellectual challenges such as appropriately finding and using information. Creating spaces for reflection can help learners adjust to those intellectual challenges and provides a way for learners to incorporate their own experiences with new information in a meaningful way. Here are some key points to take away:

- Providing intentional opportunities for reflection helps learners develop the ability to look for contextual cues to deepen their learning experiences.
- Everyone brings unique assumptions to learning experiences. Reflecting on these assumptions helps learners solve problems in new ways.
- Working with learners to recognize how their own varied experiences contributes to their intellectual development empowers them to create new connections.

The Epistemological Reflection Model provides some insights into how working with learners can develop stronger abilities to solve intellectual problems. The next chapter will look at a model that more fully explores the opportunities for working with learners as partners to address information problems.

References

Baxter Magolda, Marcia B. 1992. *Knowing and Reasoning in College: Gender-Related Patterns in Students' Intellectual Development.* Jossey-Bass Higher and Adult Education Series. San Francisco: Jossey-Bass.

de jesus, nina. 2014. "The Filter Bubble Is a Misguided, Privileged Notion." *Geek Feminism Blog,* February 27. http://geekfeminism.org/.

Eckel, Edward J. 2007. "Fostering Self-Regulated Learning at the Reference Desk." *Reference and User Services Quarterly* 47 (1): 16–20.

Evans, Nancy J., Deanna S. Forney, Florence M. Guido, Lori D. Patton, and Kristen A. Renn. 2010. *Student Development in College: Theory, Research, and Practice.* 2nd ed. Jossey-Bass Higher and Adult Education Series. San Francisco: Jossey-Bass.

Howard-Hamilton, Mary F. 2003. "Theoretical Frameworks for African American Women." *New Directions for Student Services* 104:19–27.

James, Alison, and Stephen Brookfield. 2014. *Engaging Imagination: Helping Students Become Creative and Reflective Thinkers.* San Francisco: Jossey-Bass.

Oregon State University. 2016. "The Human Library at the Valley Library." OSU Libraries. http://guides.library.oregonstate.edu/.

Pariser, Eli. 2011. "Beware Online 'Filter Bubbles.'" TED Talk. http://www.ted.com/.

Person, Natalie K., and Arthur G. Graesser. 1999. "Discourse Patterns for Mediating Peer Learning." In *Cognitive Perspectives on Peer Learning,* edited by Angela M. O'Donnell and Alison King, 69–86. Mahwah, NJ: Lawrence Erlbaum.

Syracuse University Libraries. 2016. "Syracuse University's Human Library." Subject Guides. http://researchguides.library.syr.edu/.

Torres, Vasti, and Marcia Baxter Magolda. 2004. "Reconstructing Latino Identity: The Influence of Cognitive Development on the Ethnic Identity Process of Latino Students." *Journal of College Student Development* 45 (3): 333–47.

Tulis, Spencer. 2015. "Human Library." *Finger Lakes Times,* November 17. http://www.fltimes.com/.

CHAPTER 5

Developing the Learner's Voice

IN THIS CHAPTER

▷ Providing supportive learning experiences to develop interdependent learners

▷ Encouraging learners to use their own expertise in shared learning experiences

▷ Working with learners to solve problems beyond the classroom

---

A DEVELOPMENTAL CHALLENGE FOR ALL TYPES of educators is how to encourage learners to transfer what they have learned to new contexts, inside and outside the classroom. This challenge becomes especially clear as learners leave the academic environment and face more real-world questions where they need to make more complicated decisions on their own as adult learners. As they make this transition, learners need to figure out how to solve problems at home, at work, and in their community. Not only do learners at this stage need to solve problems, but also they begin to develop their own expertise and need to find ways to share the new knowledge they have. Librarians can work with learners to discover new ways of thinking about and creating information when traditionally aged high school or college students make the transition to becoming independently driven problem solvers and once adult learners are dealing with real-world problems and are developing their own voices.

The theory discussed in this chapter—the Learning Partnerships Model—builds on the Reflective Judgment and Epistemological Reflection Models discussed in chapters 3 and 4 by describing ways to encourage adult learners to develop their critical-thinking and knowledge-creation skills, especially after the completion of college. Both the Reflective Judgment Model and the Epistemological Reflection Model describe how learners perceive and work with knowledge and information at different stages of their lives. These models extend previous understandings of how people interact with knowledge by describing approaches to complex, real-world problems that vary depending on the context of the problem and the learner's background. The Learning Partnerships

Model takes those models' ideas a step further by recognizing that learners not only take in information but also begin to create their own perspectives and voice. The Learning Partnerships Model calls for a shift away from relying on experts as the primary source of knowledge and seeks to establish learning environments where learners work and learn in partnership with educators.

This chapter will look at how this model was developed, the key principles of this model, and how librarians can apply those principles within the contexts of reference, instruction, and outreach. This model has particular relevance for librarians who work with nontraditional populations or who work with adult learners. Practical strategies that emphasize ways to empower learners to share their own expertise and insights will be discussed.

Cognitive-Structural Theories as a Bridge to Other Theories

Chapters 2, 3, and 4 each introduced an intellectual development theory that described how people think and how people's thinking develops through stages. While the previous intellectual development theories focused on different populations or different contexts for observing how people respond to intellectual challenges, each of the preceding theories were based on the core idea of development stages. The Learning Partnerships Model doesn't focus on stages but rather calls for new relationships between educators and learners. Instead of relying on the traditional educational hierarchy, the Learning Partnerships Model flattens these relationships so that learners can be equal partners in their learning, thereby encouraging them to value their own thinking and approaches to solving problems.

The Learning Partnerships Model describes relationships between an educator and a learner, and suggests that learning is a relational activity. This assertion positions the Learning Partnerships Model to serve as a connecting point to learning theories educators use to generate ideas for teaching learners with a variety of backgrounds and learning preferences. Learning, information seeking, and decision making don't happen in a vacuum but instead are typically made in a social context. As a result, context and the learner's environment and background are accounted for in the Learning Partnerships Model, which also makes this model a helpful bridge to theories about personal identity and how understandings about identity develop over time. An identity theory will be discussed in chapter 6.

This model was based on research with participants after they finished college. As a result, people in the young adult stage and early to mid-career workers are the focus. The next sections will provide background information for the Learning Partnerships Model so that librarians come away with new ideas for creating services and opportunities for learners to work with each other and to recognize the knowledge contributions learners have to share.

Learning Partnerships Model

The history of the Learning Partnerships Model picks up again with research done by Marcia Baxter Magolda. As she was completing her initial interviews with college students from Miami University, she became increasingly aware that the intellectual development skills of dealing with ambiguity and making hard decisions continued well beyond the college experience into learners' personal and work lives (Baxter Magolda 2008). To learn more about people's evolving understandings of information and knowledge, she continued her interviews after the initial five years and kept interviewing the participants for sixteen more years. Thirty-five participants remained in the study, and as a result, Baxter Magolda was able to get a picture of adult development that extended into the participants' late thirties (Baxter Magolda 2004). During these postcollege interviews, participants discussed how they approached knowledge problems in their personal and work lives. What Baxter Magolda observed was that participants began to trust their internal voices more and engaged in more independent and contextual ways of knowing in their midtwenties. By the time most of these participants were in their thirties, they more fully aligned their private and public ways of thinking and were able to make meaning in the wide range of contexts they encountered in their lives (Baxter Magolda 2008).

Baxter Magolda described these more independent and internal ways of making meaning as self-authoring abilities. She borrowed the term "self-authorship" from psychologist Robert Kegan (1994) who used it to explain how people behave as they develop their own understandings of a variety of complex problems and assume more responsibilities for their own decisions. Kegan describes adult learners' journey from being dependent on others for information and ideas to being independent in their quest for understanding and to being interdependent on others as they seek out more nuanced ways to address complex problems (see figure 5.1). Baxter Magolda created the Learning

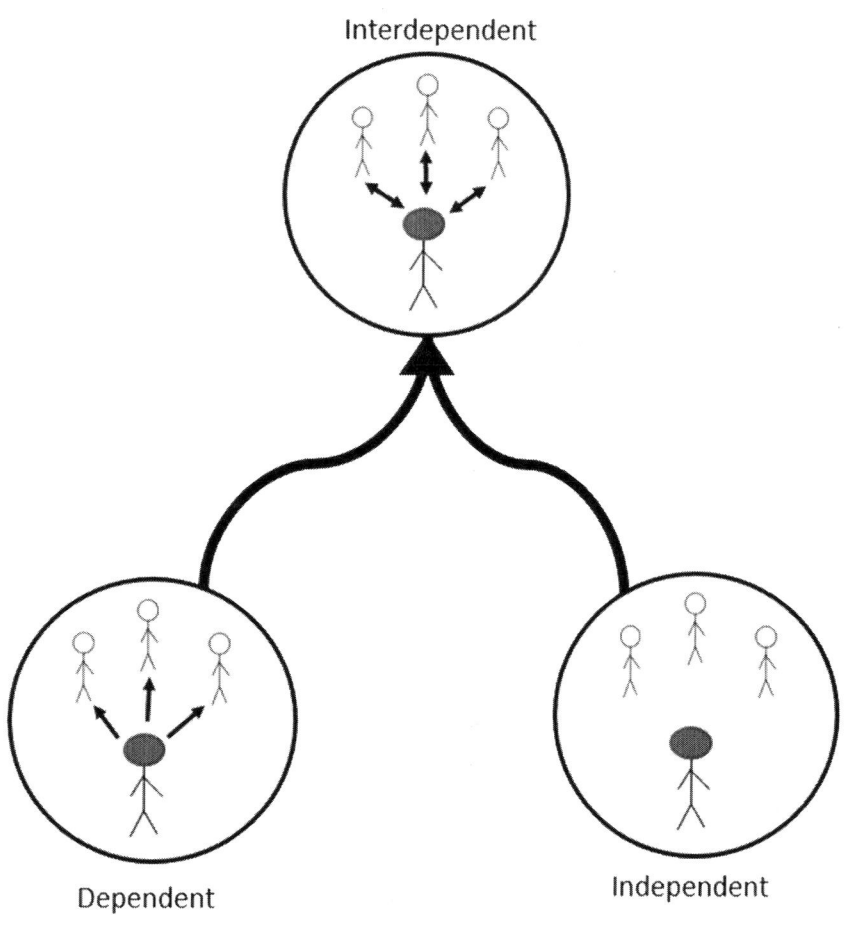

Figure 5.1. Growth in self-authoring from dependence to independence and to interdependence. *Adapted from Kegan 2004.*

Partnerships Model to propose a way to support and challenge learners to become more comfortable with their own internal identities and ways of knowing as they develop strategies for seeking information interdependently (Baxter Magolda 2004).

The Learning Partnerships Model brings together two perspectives (see figure 5.2). The model combines the challenges that an individual faces when learning new things and addressing complicated problems with a system of support for learning how to deal with those problems. The "challenges" part of the model encourages people who are dependent on outside authorities to take more responsibility for creating their own views and to seek out information that makes sense based on different contexts. On the flip side, the "support" part of the model recognizes that while external supporters or educators may be needed to help with cognitive growth, these educators are not simply bestowing expertise or delivering content. The support system is made up of educators (a term that is meant as broadly as possible) who value and respect their learners and who will work with their learners to model new ways of solving problems and creating knowledge (Baxter Magolda 2004).

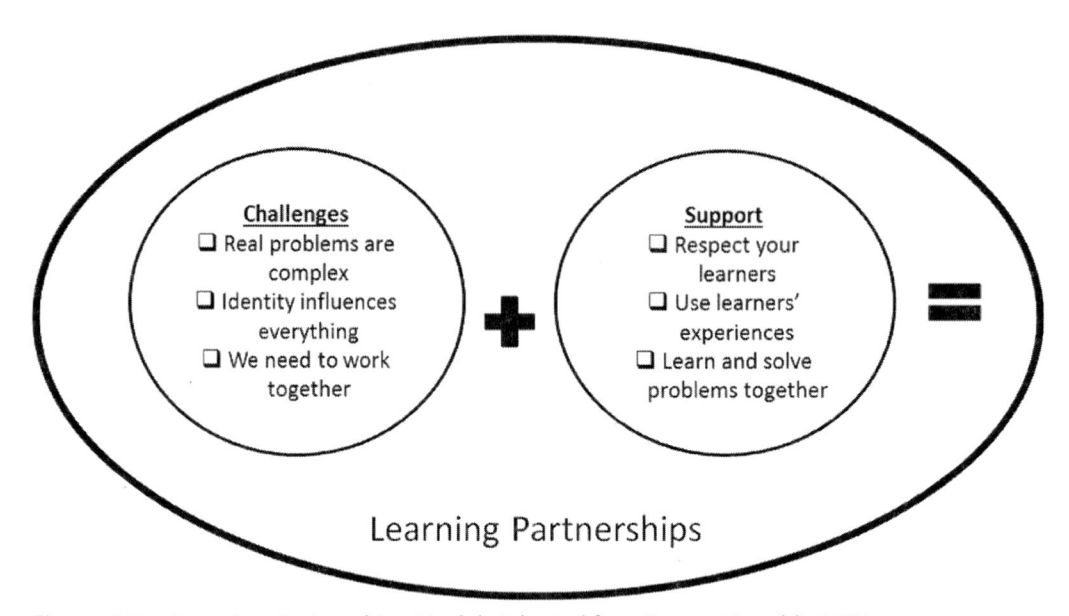

Figure 5.2. Learning Partnerships Model. *Adapted from Baxter Magolda 2004.*

The Learning Partnerships Model acknowledges that no one learns in isolation, and increasingly few people work individually to solve difficult problems. Learners who begin to appreciate the complexity of the problems they face will be more likely to look for more nuanced solutions. Similar to the Epistemological Reflection Model, the Learning Partnerships Model suggests that learners who understand how their identity and background experiences influence the ways they make meaning will be better positioned to consider a wider range of information sources and options for solving problems.

Educators (including librarians) have a role to play in how learners approach these problems. Baxter Magolda suggests that the way educators view their learners and structure learning experiences impacts learners' ability to apply what they have learned to problems beyond the classroom or library. The Learning Partnerships Model proposes that educators encourage learners' ability to create knowledge by taking into consideration learners' values, backgrounds, and personal experiences within a respectful learning environment. Educators can also help their learners develop independent thinking skills by revealing that they themselves don't have all the answers and that learning happens by solving problems together. Educators should model a variety of approaches to solving problems and give multiple opportunities to practice dealing with complex problems within formal settings because, after students complete high school or college, support structures for promoting independent and interdependent growth are less intentional. The learner needs to create their own support system and rely on their own approaches for dealing with information challenges (Baxter Magolda 2004).

Similar to the earlier emphasis on transition points in the Intellectual and Ethical Development Theory and the recognition of the importance of having uncomfortable experiences in the Reflective Judgment Model, Baxter Magolda argues that in order for people to develop self-authoring skills, they need to be presented with challenges that encourage the growth of these skills (2008). These challenges can either come in the form of problem-based learning examples, actual community or professional problems, or input from people who share different perspectives. When learners aren't presented with sufficient challenges or don't choose to engage with questions outside of their comfort zone, the development of these skills may be delayed or absent.

One example of the delay of these problem-solving skills was demonstrated by the recent Project Information Literacy study introduced in chapter 3. More than a quarter of the young adults interviewed felt ill prepared to ask their own questions in order to solve problems in their personal and professional lives (Head 2016). These findings indicate that participants had not yet developed self-authoring skills. Participants identified several factors that inhibited their ability to think for themselves and ask harder questions: a high student-to-professor ratio, the institutional culture, and the specific disciplinary curriculum at their colleges and universities. When thinking about this problem through the lens of the Learning Partnerships Model, it appears that not only were elements of the support side missing but also students weren't being challenged enough. In addition, the Project Information Literacy researchers suggested that students were often more focused on grades than on achieving true, deeper forms of knowing (Head 2016).

In contrast, when Jane Pizzolato (2003) interviewed high-risk college students from underrepresented populations to see how well the ideas of self-authoring and learning partnerships applied to them, she found that because of the early life challenges they faced, these students had developed self-authoring abilities much earlier than their more privileged peers. Challenges came in the form of needing to pay for college, support dependents, and leave home as a first-generation college student. Learners who have faced these types of challenges make up a significant portion of today's college student body. A National Center for Educational Statistics report found that 74 percent of 2011–2012 undergraduates were considered nontraditional because they had at least one characteristic from a list of criteria that included supporting a dependent, delaying the start of their college education, or working full time (Walton Radford, Cominole, and Skomsvold 2015).

The Learning Partnerships Model situates educators at a helpful junction for working with people who come from a wide range of backgrounds. Rather than treating students with a one-size-fits-all approach, the Learning Partnerships Model allows learners to build on their personal experiences to work together with their peers and educators to continue to develop their own internal voice.

You may be wondering if the Learning Partnerships Model really addresses intellectual development. While it has elements of intellectual development in the way it proposes valuing information sources and developing decision-making skills, this model serves as a bridge to other learning models and theories, particularly those that use constructivist approaches, such as Vygotsky's Social Development Theory. Psychologist Lev Vygotsky argued that learning was based on social relationships. As a result, he suggested that understanding how social interactions work in a particular setting has to happen before the more cognitive elements of learning new information can occur. He also proposed that learning is collaborative and that everyone can be both a teacher and a learner (Murphy, Mufti, and Kassem 2008; Learning-Theories.com 2014). The Learning Partnerships Model shares those foundational principles but was established within the lens of intellectual development because of its focus on how learners process and use new information to create their own ideas and voice.

The Learning Partnerships Model also serves as a bridge to identity development theories because one of the challenges suggested by this model is that identity influences everything including the way information is selected and processed on the path to developing an understanding of one's own voice. Suggestions and strategies for providing opportunities for learners to practice their self-authoring skills within library settings will be explored next.

Applying the Learning Partnerships Model to the Library Context

Baxter Magolda observed that some of the participants in her study were caught in a cycle of trying to do exactly what was expected of them in their careers or their family relationships rather than exploring a path based on their own informed choices (Evans et al. 2010). As a result, the core goal of the Learning Partnerships Model is to find ways to develop learners' voices—particularly adult learners. Educator Jack Mezirow (2000) believes that adult learners have to undergo a transformation in the way they learn and acquire information to keep up with the rapid changes in our society and workplaces. Librarians can be part of this learning transformation by moving beyond the mechanics of helping learners find information to providing spaces, forums, and instructional opportunities for interacting with the ideas in the information they find. This section will explore how librarians can encourage learners to practice becoming partners in their own learning by giving them more control over reference interactions, crafting problem-based learning activities, and developing ways to share ideas and information publicly.

Reference Consultations and the Learning Partnerships Model

The Learning Partnerships Model encourages educators and learners to work together to find ways to develop learners' voices in meaningful settings. Librarians can value learners' previous backgrounds and interests by drawing on examples from everyday life (see the Real-Life Instruction Example). Starting a reference consultation by establishing research as a nonthreatening activity with which the learner already has some experience is one way to encourage learners to try out their own ideas.

REAL-LIFE INSTRUCTION EXAMPLE

If I am going over the basics (and the importance) of keyword searching, I always attempt to frame it within something that the student is interested in, often without explaining at the outset that we're discussing "research." For example, I might have a student outline the process of making the decision to buy a new phone, asking questions such as, What do you think about when purchasing a phone? and, What kind of information do you need before you make this decision?

—Chris Nylund, Middle Georgia State University, personal communication, February 4, 2016

Another way to apply the Learning Partnerships Model is to move the librarian behind the scenes and promote opportunities for students to be leaders in providing peer reference services. Several libraries have established programs that allow learners to be active partners within reference settings, thereby providing these learners with the practice they need to develop into independent researchers. The first example comes from Gustavus Adolphus College where they use undergraduate peer-reference tutors to deliver reference services, particularly late at night (Twait 2015). Librarians at Gustavus Adolphus have found this approach not only gives students practice answering reference questions but also provides an opportunity to practice reflective listening and being empathetic with their fellow students who are experiencing library anxiety and feelings of low research self-efficacy.

A similar program is in place at the University of British Columbia (Mitchell and Bell 2012). However, at the University of British Columbia Library, students deliver many of the services at the reference desk, and they are also involved in instruction within their learning commons. Not only do the student workers receive technical training, but also they are encouraged to see themselves as a vital part of the library. Because it is often easier for students to approach their peers with questions, these students are well positioned to be ambassadors for library services. Giving student workers the experience of going out into the learning commons and demonstrating tools such as Zotero, Excel, or specific databases empowers them to be engaged in a more holistic approach to providing reference services.

An alternative example of turning more control of the reference experience over to learners comes from a project at Purdue University Libraries (Stonebraker and Zhang 2015). Realizing that many undergraduate students turn to their peers for help rather than to librarians, and recognizing that many questions are about specific classes or instructional situations that librarians may not know about, librarian software developers decided to try out an approach students are likely familiar with based on searching for help within online communities such as Ask.com or Yahoo Answers. They created a crowdsourced, web-based help system called CrowdAsk to see if students might use such a system to both ask and answer library-related research questions. Users can vote on popular responses, and the system administrators assign badges to students who answer questions particularly well. These interactive and gaming elements are meant to incentivize the process of creating user-generated content. At this point, CrowdAsk has only been used in assigned classes, but future iterations may result in students more voluntarily engaging in similar online communities. It remains to be seen whether the librarian involvement that still takes place behind the scenes helps or hinders the uptake of this type of direct student involvement in answering reference questions.

In summary, some reference strategies that give learners directed practice with the reference experience include

- starting with simple research examples common to learners' everyday experiences;
- training student workers to directly deliver reference to their peers; and
- providing structures for learners to practice responding to research-based questions in a crowdsourced environment.

Depending on your work context, some of these examples may feel like more of a stretch than others. The Learning Partnerships Model is centered in valuing the experiences that all learners bring. The expertise you bring as a librarian is one type of experience; think about what other experiences your community of learners brings that you can capitalize on so that a wider variety of voices are included at your library.

Library Instruction and the Learning Partnerships Model

One of the foundational assumptions about learning in the Learning Partnerships Model is that developing knowledge is a shared activity between learners, their peers, and educators because authority and expertise don't just belong to external authorities (Baxter Magolda 2004). Library instruction settings provide natural opportunities for learners to begin to see themselves as authors and creators, but some shifts in how librarians view authority may be required to make room for learners' expertise. The Association of College and Research Libraries' (ACRL) Framework for Information Literacy for Higher Education (2016) emphasizes the contextual nature of authority. Explicitly exploring and discussing the authority of an instructor in a classroom is one way for learners to conceptualize the interdependence of authority. Some practice and experimentation on the part of librarians may be needed to make space for these shared learning experiences. Librarians' expertise is still valued in this model, but more of the work shifts to designing learning experiences that facilitate meaningful ways for learners to recognize their own authority.

One instruction activity to help learners to think of themselves as individuals who have expertise to share is writing or editing *Wikipedia* articles. The Wikipedia Education Program (https://outreach.wikimedia.org/wiki/Education) has resources and best practices for helping instructors get started with using *Wikipedia*. In addition, there are many examples of class-based *Wikipedia* projects in the literature (Konieczny 2016). Here are two examples of how *Wikipedia* could be used in an instruction session.

Writing full *Wikipedia* articles on a specific subject area the class is studying is one way to encourage learners to develop their own voices. For example, at the University of British Columbia, students either create or expand on *Wikipedia* articles about specific books they are studying in class (Beasley-Murray 2015). Because *Wikipedia* articles undergo outside review by *Wikipedia*'s editors (and anyone else on the web who wants to provide input), students learn to revise and write for an audience outside of the classroom using language and sources that are appropriate for that audience. Rather than focusing on subject-specific knowledge, a second approach to using *Wikipedia* is as a tool to develop real-life research skills. Students at Montana State University find *Wikipedia* entries called "stubs" that are too short and are missing key information, and then they find information and sources to expand the stubs (Kittrell 2015). Learners must use a variety of sources, and they learn how to document and summarize those sources appropriately.

The advantage of creating writing projects in *Wikipedia* is that learners get to see their own work publicly displayed in a source they themselves use on a regular basis. Instead of feeling as if their work exists only for a single teacher to see, they can readily grasp how their work contributes to a project that is useful for many people. In addition, writing and editing in *Wikipedia* gives learners the opportunity to receive feedback from a new audience and to learn how to adapt their writing to new contexts.

Librarians can also work with advanced learners, such as graduate students, to encourage the development of their authoring skills in realistic settings. In shorter sessions such as a literature review workshop or a graduate-level one-shot session, it may be appropriate to briefly introduce how to find and choose scholarly sources. But then follow that exercise with an activity that can encourage the development of realistic authoring skills. Ask learners to brainstorm a range of contexts in which they might need to use sources. Some examples might include grant proposals, conference presentations, journal articles, book chapters, and presentations to the public. Next, ask learners to discuss in pairs who the audience is for each of those presentation contexts. Direct learners to generate one or two strategies or techniques they should use to present the information from a source to that particular audience. For example, when using a source in a presentation, a graph summarizing relevant data points might be most meaningful, whereas when using a source in a grant proposal, a brief summary of the impacts on policies or funding might be most appropriate. If you have enough time, ask learners to find one source that is relevant for their topic and then create an audience-appropriate summary of the source for three different contexts. See table 5.1 for an illustration of how to introduce this activity.

If you have more time to work with advanced learners, either in a term-long class or in a longer workshop setting, another realistic professional exercise is to ask learners to create an individual development plan (IDP). IDPs are commonly used by government agencies but can be useful even for learners who are not considering working for the government because the purpose of an IDP is to create a plan for your career goals. Creating an IDP can happen over the course of three activities. Learners can begin by researching what professionals in their target field actually do. Finding this information could require students not just to search for relevant blogs or articles but also to find someone in their field to interview. Once learners have a better sense of the day-to-day activities of professionals in their field, ask them to research what training or development activities are available to workers in this field. Learners could explore conferences, certificate programs, training manuals, workshop opportunities, and online learning options to discover the

Table 5.1. Audience analysis exercise sample handout

	NAME OF CONTEXT 1:	NAME OF CONTEXT 2:	NAME OF CONTEXT 3:
Audience?			
Writing strategy or technique?			
Audience appropriate summary of the source			

range of training opportunities that are available. Ask learners to reflect on what combination of these activities might work best for them and to estimate what a realistic range of activities might include over the course of one year. Finally, ask learners to create a few career goals. You could either focus on goals for one year or include a combination of shorter and longer term goals. Many examples of IDPs exist on the web. Encourage learners to view examples to help them create their own IDPs using established practices and also to demonstrate the relevance of this exercise for their future work.

Career exploration projects are not just for graduate students. Librarians at the Harrisburg University of Science and Technology worked with undergraduate students on an I-Search project, which was focused on helping students prepare for internships (Adams and Olivetti 2012). Part of this assignment included a research log to encourage students to track the range of available resources, to reflect on how they might use those resources, and to think critically about their options.

The Learning Partnerships Model encourages incorporating realistic and meaningful authoring exercises within safe spaces. Demonstrating that you are willing to learn from your students and providing real problems, such as how to pursue professional development opportunities, helps to stretch learners' ability to address these types of problems on their own. In summary, some instructional strategies that give learners a chance to practice creating realistic products include the following:

- Writing in public venues such as *Wikipedia*
- Summarizing and writing for a range of audiences (not just scholarly audiences)
- Developing realistic goals for themselves as a member of a targeted profession

Library Outreach and the Learning Partnerships Model

Library outreach events, particularly in public libraries, lend themselves particularly well to new interpretations of who experts are and provide spaces for new voices to be heard. Library outreach activities can bring together community members to solve everyday problems. Libraries can also showcase the interesting ideas and diverse viewpoints of members of their community by providing public forums for presentations and discussions. While librarians work to organize and facilitate these events, the focus is on the participants themselves and the knowledge they are developing and sharing.

One outreach example is of libraries that have built on their reputations as community gathering spaces by hosting either formal or informal TEDx-style talks. TEDx events are built on the popular TED conferences and talks but allow independent organizers to create their own version of the event. Several libraries, including Juneau (Alaska) Public Library, Butte (Montana) Public Library, and the Koprivnica Library in Croatia have held TEDx-style events. Either TEDx events can include original presentations from local community members or videos of TED talks can be shown and a facilitated time for discussion can be held afterward.

Some people have opportunities to craft their ideas into presentations and speak publicly as part of their jobs, but many do not. Giving community members the chance to develop their own voice can help them to feel empowered. In addition, hosting TEDx events can be a way to have public conversations about real problems while presenting a forum for fostering interactions for jointly solving those problems.

Another outreach example is of DIY bike-repair workshops. Corvallis-Benton County Public Library (Oregon) regularly hosts a monthlong series of DIY bike-repair and maintenance workshops with topics ranging from fixing flat tires to maintaining brakes and building bike buckets. In a city with many bikers and bike paths, the need to be able to maintain a bike is a real problem many community members face. The librarian organizing the event recognized the need to develop these skills and created a supportive environment to learn these basic bike repair and maintenance skills. Because Corvallis is a college town with regular turnover, providing a safe place for adult learners to go and practice asking questions in an unfamiliar town on a new topic matches the needs both Alison Head and Marcia Baxter Magolda identified to develop self-authoring abilities.

Key Points

Giving learners chances to develop their own voices and to practice creating realistic products provides the support and challenges they need to successfully engage with meaningful intellectual problems. Librarians can create the contexts for learners to practice these problems, but learners must be included as full partners in developing their own knowledge and understanding. Here are some key points to take away:

- Developing peer-learning and peer-teaching experiences allows learners to value their own expertise and gives authentic opportunities to share that expertise.
- Assignments and exercises with clear connections to realistic professional or personal problems provide a meaningful framework that can motivate learners to gain new knowledge.
- Opportunities for developing one's own voice not only are needed in academic settings for traditional, college-aged students but also extend throughout the lifespan.

The Learning Partnerships Model brings together concepts from intellectual, identity, and learning theories and can serve as a means of integrating several of these theories into librarians' practice. The next chapter will guide you through a key identity development theory and will discuss ways to incorporate that theory into your work as a librarian.

References

ACRL (Association of College and Research Libraries). 2016. "Framework for Information Literacy for Higher Education." January 11. http://www.ala.org/.

Adams, Nancy E., and Jennifer K. Olivetti. 2012. "Making It Better: Library and Student Services Collaboration at Harrisburg University of Science and Technology." In *Environments for Student Growth and Development: Libraries and Student Affairs in Collaboration*, edited by Lisa Janicke Hinchliffe and Melissa Autumn Wong, 57–72. Chicago: Association of College and Research Libraries.

Baxter Magolda, Marcia. 2004. "Learning Partnerships Model: A Framework for Promoting Self-Authorship." In *Learning Partnerships: Theory and Models of Practice to Educate for Self-Authorship*, edited by Marcia B. Baxter Magolda and Patricia M. King, 37–62. Sterling, VA: Stylus.

———. 2008. "Three Elements of Self-Authorship." *Journal of College Student Development* 49 (4): 269–84.

Beasley-Murray, Jon. 2015. "Write a Featured Article." Wikimedia Outreach. Last updated October 8. https://outreach.wikimedia.org/.

Evans, Nancy J., Deanna S. Forney, Florence M. Guido, Lori D. Patton, and Kristen A. Renn. 2010. *Student Development in College: Theory, Research, and Practice.* 2nd ed. Jossey-Bass Higher and Adult Education Series. San Francisco: Jossey-Bass.

Head, Alison J. 2016. "Staying Smart: How Today's Graduates Continue to Learn Once They Complete College." Project Information Literacy Research Report, University of Washington, Seattle, January 5. http://papers.ssrn.com/.

Kegan, Robert. 1994. *In Over Our Heads: The Mental Demands of Modern Life.* Cambridge, MA: Harvard University Press.

Kittrell, Edis. 2015. "Extend a Stub." Wikimedia Outreach. Last updated October 8. https://outreach.wikimedia.org/.

Konieczny, Piotr. 2016. "Teaching with Wikipedia in a 21st-Century Classroom: Perceptions of Wikipedia and Its Educational Benefits." *Journal of the Association for Information Science and Technology* 67 (7): 1523–34.

Learning-Theories.com. 2014. "Social Development Theory (Vygotsky)." Learning Theories, July 23. http://www.learning-theories.com/.

Mezirow, Jack. 2000. *Learning as Transformation: Critical Perspectives on a Theory in Progress.* 1st ed. Jossey-Bass Higher and Adult Education Series. San Francisco: Jossey-Bass.

Mitchell, Julie, and Margot Bell. 2012. "Common Ground: UBC Library and Student Development in the Chapman Learning Commons." In *Environments for Student Growth and Development: Libraries and Student Affairs in Collaboration*, edited by Lisa Janicke Hinchliffe, and Melissa Autumn Wong, 151–64. Chicago: Association of College and Research Libraries.

Murphy, Lisa, Emmanuel Mufti, and Derek Kassem. 2008. *Education Studies: An Introduction.* Berkshire, UK: Open University Press.

Pizzolato, Jane Elizabeth. 2003. "Developing Self-Authorship: Exploring the Experiences of High-Risk College Students." *Journal of College Student Development* no. 44 (6): 797–812.

Stonebraker, Ilana, and Tao Zhang. 2015. "CrowdAsk: Crowdsourcing Reference and Library Help." In *Reimagining Reference in the 21st Century*, edited by David A. Tyckoson and John G. Dove, 285–94. Charleston Insights in Library, Archival, and Information Sciences. West Lafayette, IN: Purdue University Press.

Twait, Michelle. 2015. "Peer Reference Tutoring." In *Reimagining Reference in the 21st Century*, edited by David A. Tyckoson and John G. Dove, 199–206. Charleston Insights in Library, Archival, and Information Sciences. West Lafayette, IN: Purdue University Press.

Walton Radford, Alexandria, Melissa Cominole, and Paul Skomsvold. 2015. "Demographic and Enrollment Characteristics of Nontraditional Undergraduates: 2011–12." National Center for Educational Statistics, NCES 2015025, September 9. http://nces.ed.gov/.

CHAPTER 6

Understanding How Sense of Self Changes over Time

IN THIS CHAPTER

▷ Exploring one model of how identity development occurs
▷ Creating opportunities to encourage and support learner identity development

---

WHO AM I? What do I believe and why? What do I want in my life? Identity consists of many elements: racial, ethnic and cultural heritage, religious practices, moral values and beliefs, and interests and hobbies. Our sense of self continues to develop over our entire lives, but there are life stages associated with particular bursts of growth. Most of the ideas in this chapter were developed from research focused on traditional college-age learners and are commonly studied and applied in higher education, so academic librarians may find them particularly helpful. However, public librarians and school librarians may also notice learners working through changes in how they see themselves and others, how they apply their beliefs in their behaviors, and how they make choices about their future and their values. Even older adults may discover new interests or beliefs later in life, as they reflect on their experience in new ways.

Evidence of identity development sometimes hides in plain sight in the library. For example, students struggling with a research paper might also be on the verge of changing their major, as they feel overwhelmed by a subject they thought they loved. The LGBTQ books stacked in a far corner of the library may have been squirreled away by a person coming to terms with their sexuality or gender. The patrons in rages at the circulation desk over books they swear they already turned in may be learning to effectively manage their emotions. Understanding identity development can help librarians to better understand their users, to build empathy for individual interactions, and also to improve services. The theory described in this chapter—Arthur Chickering and Linda Reisser's Seven Vectors of Identity Development—builds on the models described in previous chapters. As the Reflective Judgment, Epistemological Reflection, and Learning Partnerships Models described how to support learners at various stages of life, both in and outside the classroom, the Seven Vectors provide context for the life changes that learners may be experiencing.

This chapter will discuss a theory that describes how a learners' identities change as they learn and grow. This chapter will also provide concrete examples of how librarians can use this theory to support learners throughout this process.

Theories of Identity Development

Theories about how human identity develops can be traced back to the work of Sigmund Freud, whose psychoanalytic work identified stages of human development tied to the sexual drive, or psychosexual development. Others have extended these ideas into cognitive, social, and other forms of development. Identity development theories, sometimes also called psychosocial theories, tend to propose that identity becomes increasingly complex over time, through interactions with others (Torres, Jones, and Renn 2009). You may have studied researchers such as Freud and Erikson at some stage of your academic career. This chapter will briefly touch on their work to provide some context. Much of this chapter focuses on the work of Arthur Chickering and Linda Reisser, who built on the work of earlier identity development theorists to describe the identity development of college students. Although this work is focused on identity development during a particular life stage, lessons from this theory can be applied to library learners of many different ages.

The History of Identity Development Theories

As noted above, these identity theories of development originated with the work of Sigmund Freud. Freud proposed that children progress through stages focused on different bodily functions or areas. These psychosexual stages moved from the oral period, focused on food and suckling, all the way up to the postadolescent genital period. In this stage, adults must resolve the Oedipus complex in order to become a fully realized adult (Kahn 2002). Although our contemporary focus on evidence-based practice in mental health has moved far from Freud's original work, these ideas continue to inform thought in these areas.

Erik Erikson studied with Freud's daughter Anna and was heavily influenced by Freud's psychosexual stages. Erikson proposed eight "ages" of man, each characterized by a central struggle between two competing qualities. These are shown in figure 6.1. For example, the first age is characterized by *basic trust versus basic mistrust*, as infants must come to accept that their mother will return when she leaves the room (Erikson 1963). Achieving the capacity for this type of trust does not mean the child will always trust everyone but simply means the child has developed the ability to exercise this trust as appropriate. Children who do not overcome their mistrust will be unable to proceed to the challenge of the next age. So, like psychosexual development, the eight ages can be seen as an arc that progresses somewhat linearly toward an ultimate goal of maturity.

Ego integrity vs. despair

Generativity vs. stagnation

Intimacy vs. isolation

Identity vs. role confusion

Industry vs. inferiority

Initiative vs. guilt

Autonomy vs. shame, doubt

Basic trust vs. mistrust

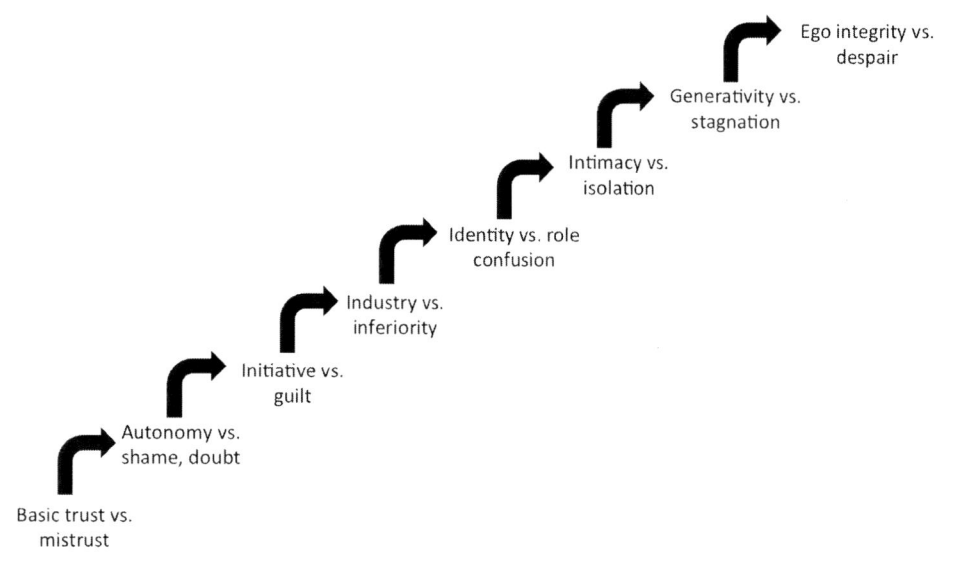

Figure 6.1. The eight ages of man, Erik Erikson, 1963

Erikson's ages of identity versus role confusion and intimacy versus isolation are generally considered the work of adolescence and early adulthood. *Identity versus role confusion* describes the process as young people not only navigate the competing desires to fit in but also become autonomous individuals. The following age, *intimacy versus isolation* is characterized by the exploration for sexual and romantic partnership. Arthur Chickering took those periods as the focus of his original research in the 1950s and 1960s, when he interviewed, tested, and reviewed diary entries of students at Goddard College in Vermont (Evans et al. 2010). The seven vectors he developed, and later revised in collaboration with Linda Reisser in the 1990s, describe seven areas of growth that seemed to be common among students he interviewed. This theory has proven remarkably tenacious and remains widely used by student affairs professionals today. As explored below, this identity theory can be applied in libraries, and not only with college-aged students.

Overview of Chickering and Reisser's Seven Vectors

Chickering and Reisser identified seven vectors where students showed a great deal of growth between starting and finishing college. The vectors are as follows:

- developing competence
- managing emotions
- moving through autonomy toward interdependence
- developing mature interpersonal relationships
- establishing identity
- developing purpose
- developing integrity

Note that each vector uses the gerund, for example, "moving" or "establishing," to indicate an ongoing development rather than a complete achievement. In contrast with linear models of development such as Erikson's, Chickering and Reisser's model does not suggest that each stage can be fully accomplished and surpassed. For example, even mature adults may struggle with developing competence or managing emotions in certain circumstances. The seven vectors are also purposefully ambiguous about the pathway of progression. Although growth in some vectors is likely to happen earlier than others, each individual's movement through the vectors will be unique and may occur in an unexpected order. However, the first four vectors are considered a foundation for what institutions can do to help students develop their identity (Chickering and Reisser 1993). The three final vectors can be seen as deepening that development.

Although there are discrete elements in each vector, other elements overlap: for example, in order to develop mature interpersonal relationships, one likely needs some ability to manage one's emotions. This suggests that an event or activity may inspire growth in multiple areas for an individual. Chickering and Reisser give little guidance about how to measure growth in each vector. Because identity development is so individual, it may look quite different for different people. Many of the examples they give throughout come from student self-reflections, suggesting that individuals may be the most able to look back and see their own growth. Nonetheless, the seven vectors provide a useful means to walk through issues that many adolescents and young adults struggle with, both in college and outside of academic environments. The following sections will describe each vector in greater detail.

Developing Competence

Most students come to college to become proficient in a particular field or set of skills. Much of the work of the university, and of the library in particular, supports students in developing competence. Chickering and Reisser note that competence can be intellectual, physical or manual, or interpersonal, and students will develop in all three areas, as well as in their general sense of their own competence (see figure 6.2).

As noted above, *intellectual competence* is the primary stated aim of most colleges or universities (see table 6.1). For example, at Oregon State University, where the authors of this book work, the mission states, "As a land grant institution committed to teaching, research, and outreach and engagement, Oregon State University promotes economic, social, cultural, and environmental progress for the people of Oregon and the world. This

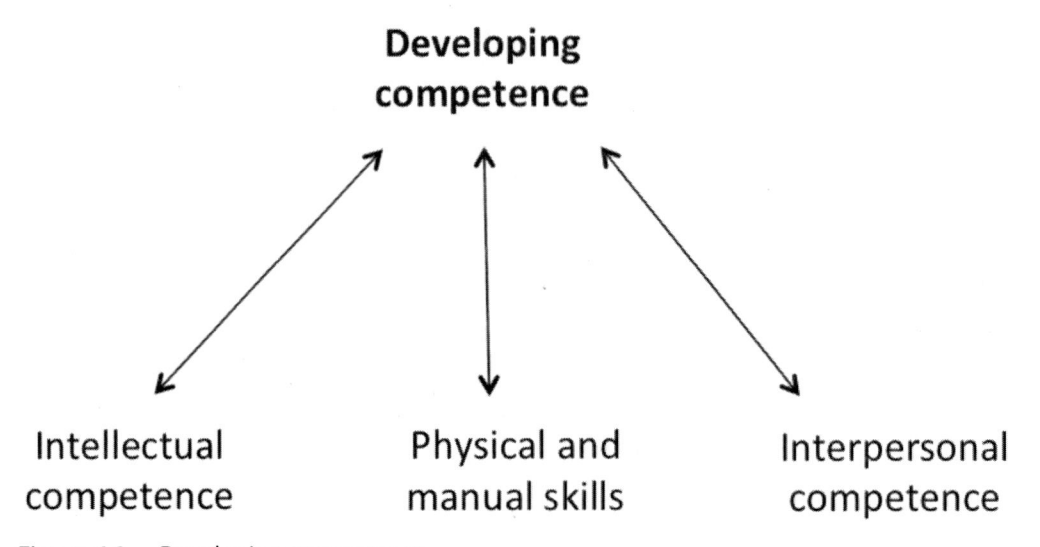

Figure 6.2. Developing competence

Table 6.1. Developing competence in a library setting

MARKERS OF PROGRESS/ AREAS FOR GROWTH	LIBRARY CONNECTIONS
Intellectual competence	Access to subject-specific information Study skills and habits Skills for lifelong learning (e.g., citation)
Physical and manual skills	Locating a book in the stacks Browsing a shelf for relevant material Using equipment and special materials (e.g., microfilm readers, scanners, and handling archival materials or rare books)
Interpersonal competence	Group study space Collaboration software (e.g., Zotero) Peer education or peer reference

mission is achieved by producing graduates competitive in the global economy, supporting a continuous search for new knowledge and solutions and maintaining a rigorous focus on academic excellence." Intellectual competence is a clearly stated objective not only for students but also for research and teaching faculty members, who are expected to create new and useful knowledge.

However, as Chickering and Reisser acknowledge, there is no universal consensus on what intellectual competence means (Chickering and Reisser 1993). The Association of American Colleges and Universities has identified four essential learning outcomes for undergraduates: knowledge of human cultures and the physical and natural world, intellectual and practical skills (including information literacy and critical thinking), personal and social responsibility, and integrative and applied learning (AAC&U 2014). These outcomes map to the three major areas of research that Chickering and Reisser identify. Overall, it does appear that students tend to gain subject knowledge between entering and leaving college, particularly within their major (Pascarella and Terenzini 2005).

Libraries of all types contribute to learners' intellectual competence. As students navigate assignments designed to build their subject expertise, they may interact with library collections, ask reference questions, or come to a workshop to learn specific skills. Learners of all ages may come to a public library or a public university library to explore topics of interest outside any formalized learning experience. Besides providing access to subject information, as noted in chapters 2–5 libraries also provide sites for developing intellectually by learning the skills for lifelong learning, as learners observe others studying.

Physical and manual competence is generally developed through athletics and the arts. Although wellness and creativity are worthy goals on their own, the skills and habits developed through these activities can translate to other areas. For example, a student who learns to be a good sport on the soccer field may be able to bring a healthy sense of competition into the workplace. Chickering and Reisser note that this is an area of connection to other vectors: in the case of the soccer player, respecting the referee and the opposing team requires management of emotions as well (Chickering and Reisser 1993).

On the surface, it may appear that libraries offer few opportunities for developing physical and manual competence. However, even the task of accurately reading a call number and walking through the stacks to find its location represents a combination of spatial reasoning and intellectual understanding of how books are grouped. For any learner transitioning from the Dewey Decimal System to the Library of Congress classification, it may take a few tries to locate a book. Similarly, browsing the shelves for relevant materials is a combination of subject-specific knowledge and practiced physical movement. By acknowledging that these are skills to be learned, librarians can draw learners' attention to the growth they are achieving. Finally, libraries are filled with equipment and unusual materials that require specialized training and practice. Whether it is threading a microfilm reader, recognizing when archival photographs require careful handling, or properly cradling a book on a flatbed scanner, many tasks in the library require a careful eye and delicate touch.

Finally, *interpersonal competence* consists of the skills necessary to work with others. Anyone who has experienced student complaints over group project assignments has seen the importance of this competence, which includes listening and communication, the ability to stay on task, and the ability to adjust to a group. Students just beginning to develop this competence may prefer to do all work on their own, or simply give up in the face of a group member who they see as bossy. Again, the skills that support interpersonal competence support other vectors: a student who has learned to listen empathically can use that skill with romantic partners or family members as well as classmates.

Libraries support interpersonal competence in both indirect and direct ways. By providing space for group project work, such as private study rooms, the library becomes the location for students as they experiment and practice these skills. Libraries may also support some of the technologies that students use to work together, such as Zotero for sharing references. Some libraries also use peer education programs to teach or provide reference services (see chapter 4), giving learners an opportunity to teach one another. You can find other suggestions in table 6.1.

Finally, Chickering and Reisser note that students building intellectual, physical, and interpersonal competence also begin to build an overarching overall sense of competence, as they come to recognize their own capacity. With this competence comes the willingness to explore and take risks, as learners believe they can rise to the challenge of taking on new tasks and content areas.

Managing Emotions

College can be a time of new and challenging feelings. Students who are living on their own for the first time, dating and making friends with new people, and managing their time in a radically different schedule may experience conflicts and excitement they do not know how to respond to. Learning to manage emotions gives students the resilience to face new challenges and embrace new opportunities for joy and celebration. It also serves to help students navigate mental-health crises and mental illness. Chickering and Reisser suggest that students beginning college frequently struggle to manage "toxic" feelings, such as fear, anxiety, depression, guilt, shame, and aggressive anger. These feelings may arise due to academic conditions—for example, test anxiety—or in reaction to social and personal changes, such as trauma after a sexual assault. As of fall 2015, one in four American undergraduates reported receiving some mental illness diagnosis or treatment in the previous year (American College Health Association 2015). By becoming more aware of emotions, and learning to integrate their emotions, students become, overall, more able to manage their emotions (see figure 6.3).

```
        Managing
        emotions
         ↗   ↖
        ↙     ↘
Increasing        Increasing
awareness of      integration
 emotions
```

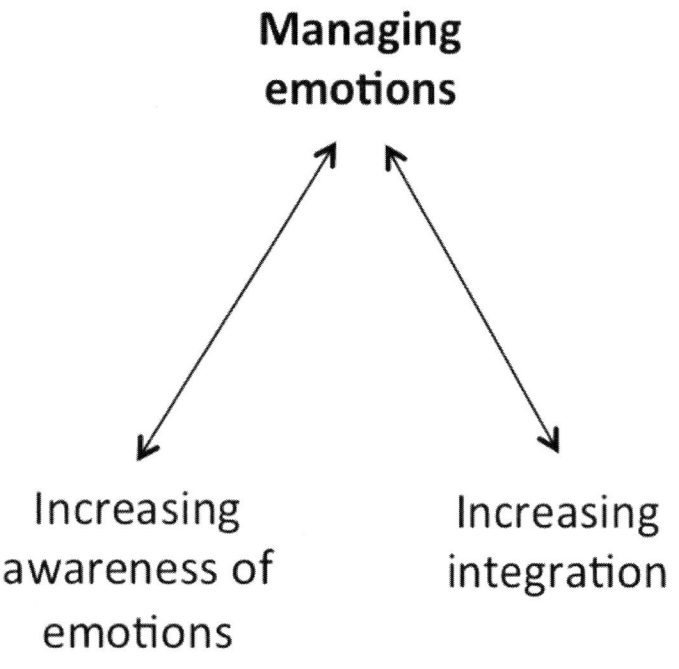

Figure 6.3. Managing emotions

Depending on their personal, cultural, and academic background, students may have a limited vocabulary for their emotions. *Becoming more aware of emotions* includes recognizing, describing, and accepting feelings. Many students feel alone in their experiences, but improved emotional literacy can help them both understand their own experience and move toward empathy by recognizing emotions in others.

Libraries can help students become more aware of their feelings simply through providing information and context. Chickering and Reisser note that students may learn about emotions from literature or textbooks, giving the example of Nathanial Hawthorne's *Scarlet Letter* as a way to reflect on feelings of lust and shame (Chickering and Reisser 1993). Displays to support annual campaigns such as Mental Health Awareness Month (May) or Suicide Prevention Awareness Month (September) can provide visual reminders to students. Even displays dedicated to common challenging situations, such as roommate conflicts or managing stress during finals, can help students recognize the feelings they are experiencing. In this work, it is important to provide easy access to campus or local resources for mental-health help. But remember, librarians are not trained mental-health workers and should not take on the role of diagnosis or treatment.

Librarians can also talk with learners about library anxiety, a sense of inadequacy with research, and reluctance to use libraries or library resources. See the Students Expressing Library Anxiety box below for real-life anxiety examples. Research on library anxiety has looked at the connections among library experience, learning style, and at-risk student groups, as well as other things (Gross and Latham 2007; Jiao, Onwuegbuzie, and Lichtenstein 1996; Kwon, Onwuegbuzie, and Alexander 2007). By acknowledging that many people experience this feeling at some time, librarians can validate the experience of nervous learners.

> ### STUDENTS EXPRESSING LIBRARY ANXIETY
>
> Even if students do not explicitly say they are afraid, you may hear them express library anxiety as hesitation to use particular tools or resistance to asking for help. The following list contains real student comments about library and research anxiety experiences they had.
>
> - "Google Scholar kind of scared me."
> - "I quickly remove myself from the library page, because it's not easy to use and not everything is readily available. So I'll start there but move out quickly."
> - "So to be quite honest, when I do research to begin with, I'm not very familiar with the library website because I haven't had any classes where the library has come to talk to us about using the library."

Integration describes the ability to recognize, regulate, and deal effectively with emotions. Chickering and Reisser note that academic skills may support emotional integration, for example, as students build test preparation skills, they can both recognize and alleviate their anxiety (Chickering and Reisser 1993). Student activism and collective action may be a way to share and act productively on anger. As movements such as Black Lives Matter raise awareness of oppression and structural violence, students may find support in speaking out and taking action.

Libraries can support emotional integration in several ways (see table 6.2). If there are opportunities to work with students as mentors, librarians can listen and help students reflect on their experiences. Libraries can provide conflict-management trainings or other emotional skill-building workshops for student workers. Libraries can also provide resources and support for student organizers. Librarians may be eligible to serve as faculty advisors for student organizations, or to attend events in solidarity.

Moving through Autonomy toward Interdependence

When Chickering first published his work, this vector was originally limited to developing autonomy as students worked to become independent from their families and other

Table 6.2. Managing emotions in a library setting

MARKERS OF PROGRESS/ AREAS FOR GROWTH	LIBRARY CONNECTIONS
Increasing awareness of emotions	Provide displays of literature and nonfiction. Train staff in mental-health first aid. Conduct reflective assessment in teaching.
Increasing integration	Provide conflict management trainings for student workers. Support student activists (e.g., as a faculty advisor for a student group).

relationships of reliance. In the 1993 revision, it was amended to focus on *inter*dependence rather than independence. This shift came partially out of recognition that gender socialization can affect ideals for attaining separation, as women may measure their own maturity in part based on the relationships they have with others and on a sense of community (Chickering and Reisser 1993). Certainly culture can also affect these aims, and this vector reflects the individualistic norms of white American culture. In the 1993 revision, the goal of moving through autonomy toward interdependence reflects three elements: emotional independence, instrumental independence, and interdependence (see figure 6.4).

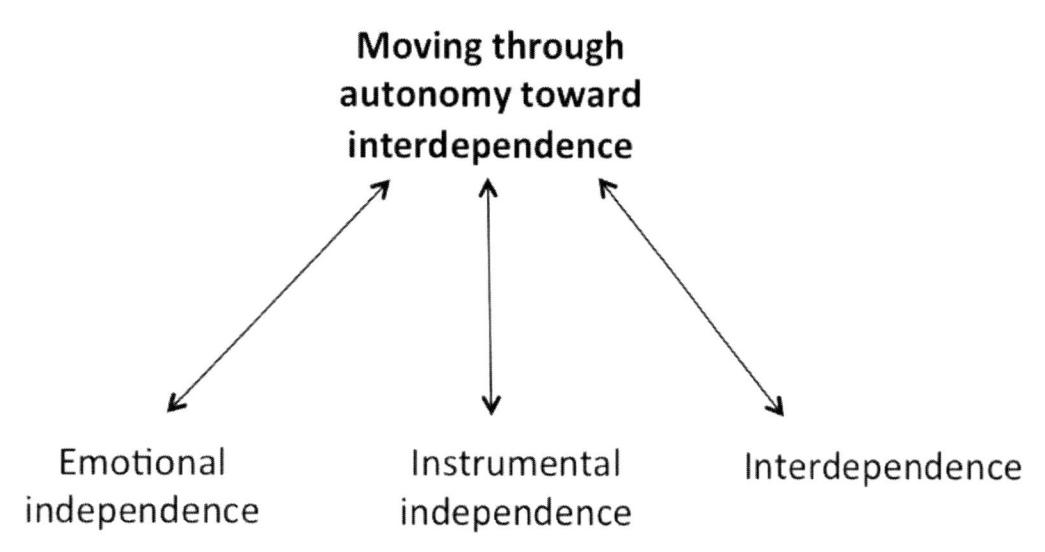

Figure 6.4. Moving through autonomy toward interdependence

Emotional independence occurs when students begin to detach from their parents or family, moving toward choosing their own network of trusted friends and advisors, and take more responsibility over their decision making. This progress point represents one aspect of interconnection between the vectors, as this independence also requires some ability to manage emotions. This area also connects with William Perry's multiplistic stage, introduced in chapter 2. As students come into their sense of self, and are better able to see the complexity of others, they can see and accept the flaws in others. During this period, trusted adults can help by listening deeply to students and by supporting them as they take responsibility for their actions. This may be complicated by familial messages, either from overbearing "helicopter parents" who cling to their children or from families that cut off support.

Instrumental independence describes self-sufficiency and problem solving. Students who have never had to do their own laundry or cook for themselves may struggle with daily tasks, on top of the new academic and social challenges they face. Time management can be a serious concern within this area. Students who have achieved this type of independence will also be able to transfer these daily skills into a new environment, whether they leave school, graduate, or transfer. For this type of growth, students need opportunities to make their own decisions, without constant monitoring.

Finally, students may move into *interdependence* when they recognize that they do need and belong to broader communities. In some cases, this may mean moving back toward their family for support and guidance, although on the student's terms. Chickering

Table 6.3. Moving through autonomy toward interdependence in a library setting

MARKERS OF PROGRESS/ AREAS FOR GROWTH	LIBRARY CONNECTIONS
Emotional independence	Caring and reflective listening during crunch times
Instrumental independence	Time management and other academic skills workshops
	Open-ended learning activities with opportunities for choice
Interdependence	Student advisory boards

and Reisser warn that autonomy may come with a sense of entitlement; true interdependence requires students to take responsibility as active members of their communities.

Librarians can support learners at all stages of moving through autonomy toward interdependence, first of all by acknowledging the autonomy of library users (see table 6.3). This may be done through caring and reflective listening, or by providing training for skills such as time management and academic reading. Library staff members who work closely with student workers may have additional opportunities to support this type of growth; motivational interviewing is one technique developed in counseling that is now frequently used in work and campus environments to support people as they choose to change their behavior (see the Motivational Interviewing box for a more in-depth explanation of this technique).

MOTIVATIONAL INTERVIEWING

Change can be hard; even when you recognize that you need to stop doing a harmful behavior, it can be extraordinarily difficult to do so. Motivational Interviewing (MI) is a technique developed by counselors working with people with substance addictions. Rather than focus on external reasons to change behavior, counselors can use MI to empower their clients to identify and build their intrinsic motivations. The four general principles of MI are to (1) express empathy, (2) develop discrepancy, (3) roll with resistance, and (4) support self-efficacy (Miller and Rollnick 2002). The sum is an approach that sidesteps conflict or top-down enforcement while building intrinsic motivation and commitment to change. Many training materials exist for implementing MI, online and in print, or you could connect with your campus counseling office to see if local training is available.

Developing Mature Interpersonal Relationships

As students meet many new people in college, they will initiate, maintain, and sometimes end many different relationships. These relationships can support—or inhibit—their growth in other areas. For example, as students navigate group assignments for a course, they may struggle to deal with feelings of anger, their own sense of competence, and how to stand up for their own opinions. Developing mature interpersonal relationships means balancing autonomy and attachment. This requires that students have tolerance and an appreciation for differences, and the capacity for intimacy (see figure 6.5).

```
        Developing mature
         interpersonal
          relationships
         ↗           ↖
        ↙             ↘
Tolerance and           Capacity for
appreciation of          intimacy
  differences
```

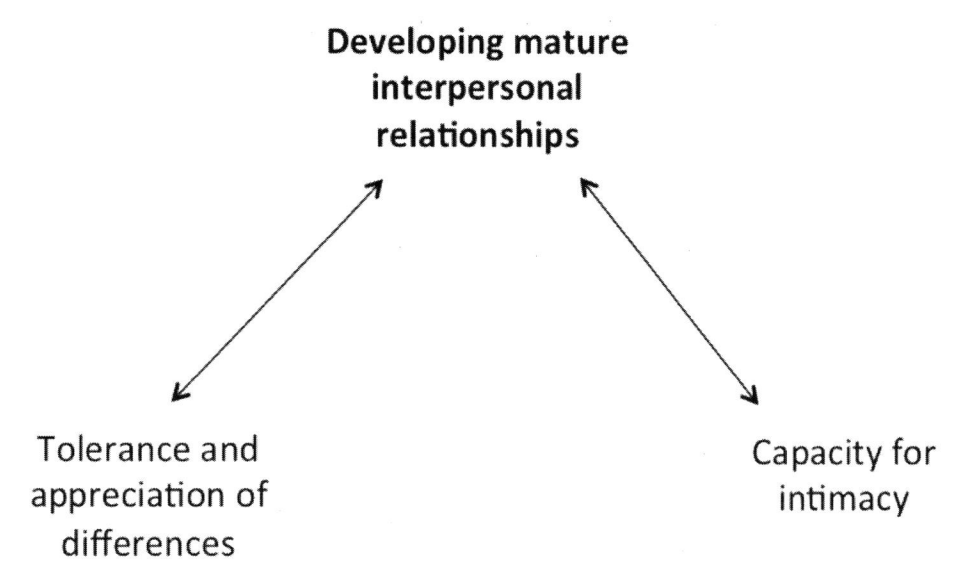

Figure 6.5. Developing mature interpersonal relationships

Tolerance means that students can recognize their own bias and begin to understand how bias is constructed and maintained. Similarly, the *appreciation of differences* requires genuine interest and openness to diversity. Chickering and Reisser discuss both elements in the spheres of intercultural and interpersonal context. So, a student may need to confront an intercultural bias against certain types of ethnic food as well as an interpersonal bias against football players. Throughout all of this work, empathy is core, as students must come to care and be curious about the experiences of others. However, Chickering and Reisser note that simply being in the presence of difference does not necessarily increase tolerance—students must actively engage with diversity and reflect on their own beliefs and values in the context of others. The ambivalent relationship between international students and domestic students on many campuses is one excellent example of this dilemma. See the Speed Friending box for an example of how the library can facilitate active engagement between international and domestic students.

SPEED FRIENDING IN THE LIBRARY

Speed friending is an event similar to speed dating, where attendees have a series of short, timed conversations with strangers. However, rather than finding a romantic partner, the goal is to meet new friends. For international students, who may find themselves largely in an enclave of other students from abroad, this is a welcome chance to mingle with domestic students. At Oregon State University, librarian Laurie Bridges works with a program manager in the international students office to arrange an event where half the attendees are international students and the other half are domestic students. Over pizza and soda, the two groups of students have a structured opportunity to have one-on-one conversations. Conversation prompts encourage cross-cultural sharing. Both international and domestic students report very positive feedback, and the series has expanded to add a session focused on welcoming international visiting scholars and faculty.

The *capacity for intimacy* entails making oneself vulnerable and taking risks in order to connect with others. As students push away from their families and find new friends, romantic partners, and mentors, they will negotiate new boundaries and expectations. Students may discover that they have different needs and values than they expected to, for example, students raised in a conservative religious environment may struggle to reconcile their queerness. Students who hide their new friends from their old friends or are completely inseparable from a new romantic partner may be struggling to be authentic and whole in their relationships. Idealizing or demonizing individuals can be a step in this process, as students may, for example, express disdain for their parents' opinions and complete adoration for an admired professor. Students will experiment throughout this time as they explore how to get their needs met.

Librarians can support students in their development along this vector through a variety of ways (see table 6.4). Chickering and Reisser note that learning about intolerance can help students build their own tolerance, so librarians can purposefully incorporate issues of diversity, inclusion, and oppression into teaching and displays. Librarians who have close mentorship relationships with learners can encourage openness in communication and reflection: students will likely have many professional relationships throughout their lives. And although the library staff may shy away from any mention of physical intimacy, librarians can partner with units on campus or in the community focused on healthy relationships to offer programming about domestic violence, conflict resolution, sexual health, or other topics.

Establishing Identity

In some ways, the establishment of identity is the overarching outcome of all of the vectors. However, the squirrely and idiosyncratic nature of identity means it can be difficult to measure, or to determine steps for. Still, Chickering and Reisser identify seven elements: comfort with body and appearance; comfort with gender and sexual orientation; sense of self in a social, historical, and cultural context; clarification of self-concept through roles and lifestyle; sense of self in response to feedback from valued others; self-acceptance and self-esteem; and personal stability and integration (see figure 6.6).

Comfort with body and appearance relates to how individuals feel about how they look and feel physically. The "freshman fifteen" is one resonant example: students may be unfamiliar with monitoring their own eating, exercise, and sleeping regimens. They may feel pressure to conform to standards of beauty or appearance, or may choose to experiment with fashion and appearance. Students may also be trying drugs, alcohol, or sexual behaviors for the first time.

Table 6.4. Developing mature interpersonal relationships in a library setting

MARKERS OF PROGRESS/ AREAS FOR GROWTH	LIBRARY CONNECTIONS
Tolerance and appreciation of differences	Provide interactive displays or programs highlighting diversity. Incorporate diverse perspectives into teaching.
Capacity for intimacy	Encourage reflective listening. Collaborate with campus partners to raise awareness.

```
                    Establishing
                     identity
Comfort with  ↗  ↗  ↑  ↖  ↖         Personal
  body and                         stability and
  appearance                        integration

Comfort with ↗                      ↖ Self-acceptance
gender and sexual                     and self-esteem
  orientation
              ↗     ↑      ↑     ↖
         Sense of self in  Clarification of  Sense of self in
         social/historical/  self-concept   response to
         cultural context  through roles   feedback from
                           and life-style  valued others
```

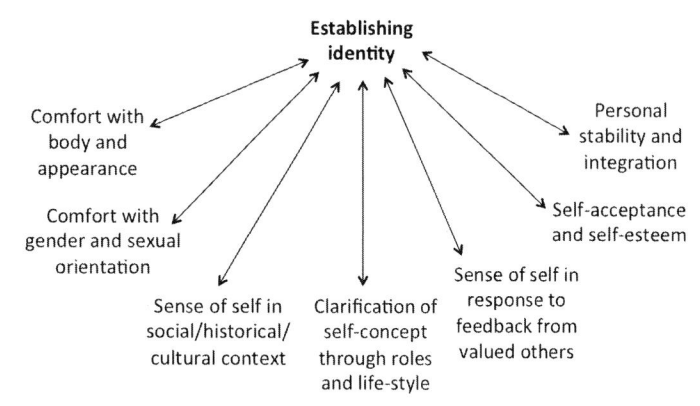

Figure 6.6. Establishing identity

Comfort with gender and sexual orientation requires that students come to terms with gender roles and stereotypes, as well as with their own romantic and sexual orientation. In an androcentric, cisnormative, and heteronormative society, this task is inherently more difficult for women, transgender, and queer students. Chickering and Reisser note that courses that focus directly on gender roles, stereotypes, and equity can help students overcome their sense of doubt or internalized sexism.

Sense of self in a social, historical, and cultural context means that individuals understand their ethnic, racial, and cultural history, practices, and community, that they "know who they are." In a white-dominated society, and particularly at majority-white institutions, students of color may particularly struggle with this element. Along with the previous element, we can see this as students come to understand their sense of identity in an intersectional way. See the box for an explanation of the term intersectionality.

WHAT IS INTERSECTIONALITY?

Intersectionality describes the ways that an individual's multiple social identities overlap and interact. Legal scholar Kimberle Crenshaw coined the term to explain how black women were marginalized both in discussions of "women's issues" and "black issues" because they face particular challenges as race and gender intersect (Crenshaw 1989). This idea has been extended in conversations of other dimensions of identity, including ability, sexual orientation, ethnicity, citizenship status, and beyond.

To be clear, this struggle isn't because students of color themselves are deficient but rather because the institutions surrounding them are less likely to recognize and support their culture, history, and social practices.

Clarification of self-concept through roles and lifestyle allows individuals to modify and adapt their identity to fit their complex experiences, rather than feeling defined by their role. Students may come into college identifying themselves as a theater kid or a cross-country runner but over time will come to recognize additional facets as they discover new hobbies, interests, and vocations. The ability to both make commitments and be flexible as circumstances change will help students make decisions to move themselves forward and cope with things beyond their control, such as a breakup or losing a job.

A *sense of self in response to feedback from valued others* will allow students to appropriately incorporate or discount criticism from outside sources. This requires a strong sense of self and ability to self-assess, as students must determine which comments are valid and how to use that information. You may recall a bad grade on an assignment when a professor simply didn't get what you were trying to say, or an argument with a friend who was unwilling to hear your negative opinion about their new girlfriend. For some people, the stakes are graver, for example, a student who comes out as genderqueer may struggle with negative feedback from friends, family, and acquaintances who refuse to use their pronouns as requested. The lesson here is not to entirely disregard or entirely absorb all feedback but to be able to hear and think reflectively about feedback.

Self-acceptance and self-esteem refers to an individual's general sense of being a good person. Students may come to college with unreasonable expectations for themselves, or with a lack of confidence in their ability to succeed. Self-acceptance and self-esteem serve us as we face challenges, make missteps, and reach for new opportunities.

Personal stability and integration describes the overall sense of self and ownership over one's identity. Although our identities include elements coming from family, religion, race, ethnicity, and other factors outside our control, ultimately all individuals are responsible for their self and their choices, and who they are.

These elements of establishing identity provide many possible points of connection with libraries. Regarding comfort with body and gender, library buildings can provide passive programming and supportive infrastructure. Libraries are often one of the only places on campus open twenty-four hours a day (although not all libraries are able to provide twenty-four-hour service), and many library workers have stories of finding used condoms, empty bottles, or snoring students in the library. Collaborations with the student health clinic can cross-promote healthy living campaigns, as many of the problem behaviors occur in libraries. Library buildings can offer gender-inclusive bathrooms, and library staff can be trained on issues facing transgender and queer students. Librarians can support students as they explore the cultural, historical, and social context of their identities by providing varied and rich examples during teaching and programming. Ultimately, the library staff can be aware that students are coming into their full sense of identity and can support that growth by providing opportunities for learning and reflection.

Developing Purpose

As Chickering and Reisser describe it, the first five vectors generally help students answer the question, who am I? The final two vectors focus on the future. Developing purpose means that students begin to consider what they want to do, personally and professionally, and how they want to live their lives. This requires consideration of vocational plans and aspirations, personal interests, interpersonal and family commitments, and intentionality (see figure 6.7).

Many students come to college with an expectation of their *vocational plans and aspirations*, but the frequency with which students change their major shows that this is also often an area of growth and change. The skyrocketing cost of college and resultant student debt, combined with an uncertain economic climate, can cause a great deal of stress and concern for the future. During their time at university, students may learn about

```
                    Developing
                     purpose
                    ↗  ↑  ↖  ↖
                   ↙  ↓    ↘    ↘
Vocational plans
and aspirations                      Intentionality
                 Personal   Interpersonal
                 interests   and family
                             commitments
```

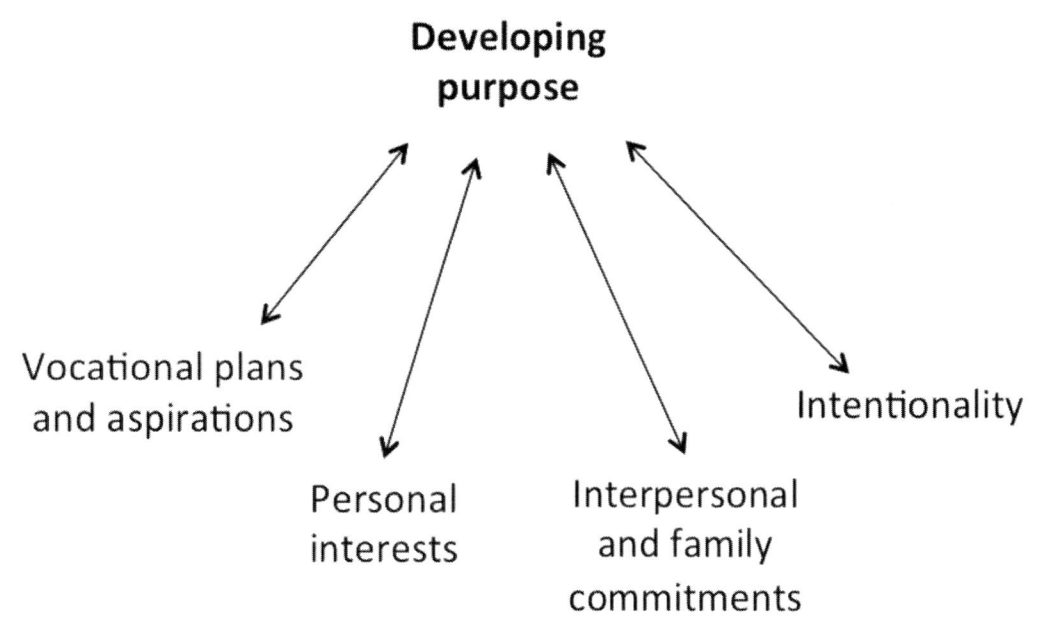

Figure 6.7. Developing purpose

careers they had not previously considered and have chances for experiential learning within their chosen field. Students may grapple with letting down family expectations to follow their own dreams; with realizing that their stated goal doesn't match their emerging personal values; or with the recognition that their strengths do not match the skillset of their desired field. Navigating these struggles with personal reflection and goal-setting can help students pursue a satisfying career path.

College is also a time when students discover new *personal interests*. The wealth of student clubs and organizations, sponsored events, and volunteer opportunities on most college campuses means that students have a lot of decisions to make about how to spend their time. Students may have practiced many sports when they were younger but need to focus on just one at the college level. As they transition into greater amounts of paid work and academic studying, they may need to clarify which hobbies they wish to commit to over time.

In addition to thinking of their own life, students likely have *interpersonal and family commitments*. Some students may have obligations to take care of aging parents, or their own children. As described in previous sections, decisions must be made about whom to spend time with and in what types of relationships. Individuals who have dated around may find themselves keen to settle down, or looking toward raising a family.

Intentionality means approaching the future with care to making purposeful choices. This doesn't mean that students must make a singular life plan and stick to it unfailingly but rather that they should approach their daily tasks and long-term goals with consideration. Intentional individuals are able to approach their future with curiosity and mindfulness, and adjust in the face of unexpected turns of event.

Libraries can help students develop their purpose through both passive and active means. For example, extracurricular reading can help learners explore a new field or interest in a low-pressure, self-directed way. Libraries can collaborate with the career center to hold programming and can provide experiential learning opportunities in the library, whether as internships, as paid positions, or through for-credit courses. As with many of the other vectors, again it is key to give learners chances to reflect and discuss their experiences.

Developing Integrity

It is difficult to always act in accordance with one's beliefs, but developing integrity means having an awareness of the connection between the two, and seeking to align them, even when it means adjusting values or behaviors. Chickering and Reisser identify the three potentially overlapping stages of this process as humanizing values, personalizing values, and developing congruence (see figure 6.8).

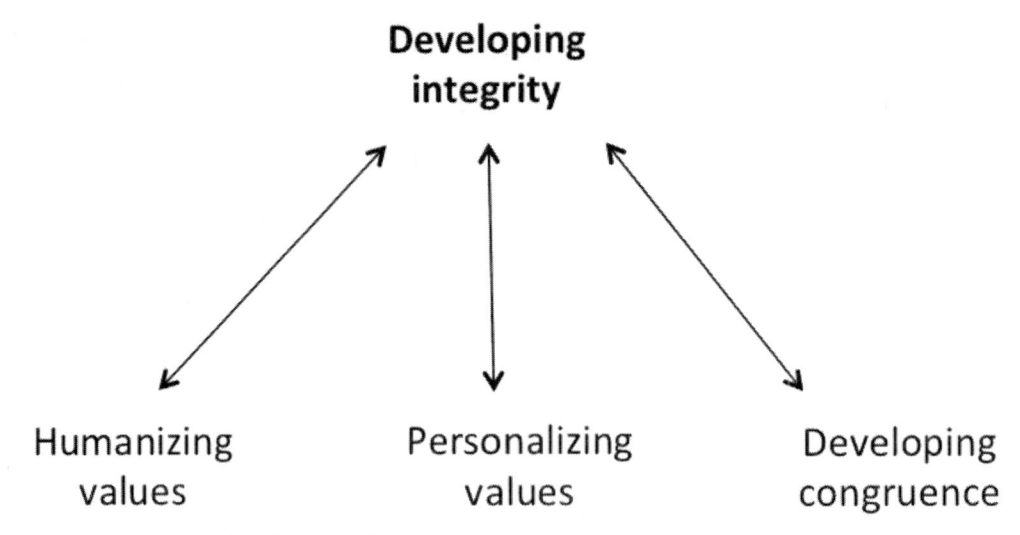

Figure 6.8. Developing integrity

Humanizing values describes the ability to adjust one's beliefs due to interactions with others. Students may come into college with dogmatic, unexamined beliefs. Through experiences with difference, particularly moments of conflict, students will be confronted with the limitations of their values and, over time, become more comfortable with ambiguity and nuance.

Personalizing values requires that individuals can describe and discuss their own beliefs and reflect on how their values apply within their own life.

When people act in accordance with their values, they are *developing congruence*. When students who value honesty choose to own up to cheating on a test, their behavior is congruent with their beliefs. This growth does not occur immediately and certainly can cause discomfort as it is enacted.

Developing integrity may be the most difficult vector for libraries to directly support. However, library workers can be explicit in talking about their shared professional values and ensuring that library policies and procedures align with those values. Work with academic integrity and discussions of plagiarism can focus on alignment of value and behavior, rather than simply enforcing rules or punishing students.

Key Influences on Student Development

In addition to the seven vectors, Chickering and Reisser identified seven key influences on student development: institutional objectives, institutional size, student-faculty relationships, curriculum, teaching, friends and student communities, and student development programs and services. Although the library may be able to contribute to some of these elements, these demand broader institutional commitment, so are not the focus here. However, it is worth considering questions such as the following: are the goals of the broader institution clearly stated and supported across campus? How does the curriculum help students develop desired behaviors and values? Do students feel personally connected to faculty and other students?

Putting Chickering and Reisser's Theory in Context

Chickering and Reisser's theory is one of the most influential in student affairs (Evans et al. 2010; Pascarella and Terenzini 2005). However, there are some notable limitations to this theory. Although the revised version acknowledges some differences in student development between genders, some racial minorities, and gay, lesbian, and bisexual students, similar to Perry's Intellectual and Ethical Development Theory described in chapter 2, Chickering and Reisser's original theory was derived from work with white, male college students. As noted earlier, an intersectional approach to identity requires understanding how elements including race, gender, and ability interact to affect development.

Although some research has validated aspects of the theory, the complex and intertwined nature of identity development makes it difficult to closely monitor. Nancy Evans and colleagues note that existing research tends to focus on a single vector, rather than the overall pattern of development (Evans et al. 2010). Given that identity development is so complex, this is a serious limitation. The seven vectors are also quite broadly defined, which can make it difficult to distinguish what precisely is included within them.

Applying the Seven Vectors of Identity Development to the Library Context

Now that you have an understanding of Chickering and Reisser's seven vectors of identity development, you can consider how you may use these ideas practically in your library work. Student affairs professionals use this theory to inform programming, individual interactions with students, and broader institutional changes, and librarians can do much the same (Evans et al. 2010). This section will discuss how to apply this theory in reference, instruction, and outreach activities in libraries. Rather than explore each vector within each area of practice, this section will highlight approaches that can apply across multiple vectors. Because of the prominence of this theory in student affairs, applying it in libraries presents opportunities to collaborate with partners across an institution, or within a broader community.

Reference and Identity Development

The idiosyncratic nature and massive scale of identity development may make it seem incompatible with fleeting reference experiences. However, there are still small choices that librarians can make, as well as structural approaches that can create an environment conducive to supporting students through their growth. Evans and colleagues note that student affairs professionals use Chickering and Reisser's theory to prepare for types of concerns that students are likely to have, for example, anticipating issues related to competency and being ready to refer students as necessary (Evans et al. 2010). In reference interactions and research consultations, librarians can similarly learn to recognize signs of growth and be ready with appropriate resources and techniques to support students at whichever phase they are found.

Developing competence is an obvious connection for library reference. For many college students, the university library will be the largest they've ever used. Academic libraries are generally organized differently than public libraries or high school libraries, may have unfamiliar types of materials, and have different expectations for use. In addition, students may find themselves needing types of information that they have not previously searched for, such as scholarly journal articles. Reference librarians can acknowledge that this requires a new set of competence and recognize students' accomplishments as they develop. One way to do this is in how research tools are organized and shared. Research guides can be presented in reference interactions as a place for students to expand subject-based or research skill competencies. The librarian can encourage students to explore the research tools specific for their discipline and emphasize that these are the tools that their professors and other experts use. Focusing on the way that professionals in a field use research skills and tools can reiterate vocational plans.

Reference interactions can be emotionally fraught for learners. Asking for help requires being vulnerable, and for learners who doubt their own abilities this admission can be taxing. Add in the pressure of completing an assignment at the last minute, and perhaps regret about poor time management, and more than just research help is needed. Librarians can offer empathy and reflective listening to surface and validate student emotions at the reference desk. Here, the work of psychologist Marshall Rosenberg around nonviolent communication can be quite useful (Rosenberg 2003). This approach to conflict asks participants to focus on making observations about a situation, articulating their own feelings and needs, and making a request to get those needs met. Although most reference interactions are not sites of conflict, this model still provides useful tips for reflective listening and engaging in empathy. Consider whether your reference training highlights the following reflective listening tips (see table 6.5). This type of listening may feel unfamiliar but has much in common with best practices for the reference interview. It is not about becoming a therapist for students but simply about listening and reflecting back what you hear. Validating a learner's feelings also does not mean badmouthing

Table 6.5. Suggestions for reflective listening

TIP	RATIONALE	EXAMPLE LANGUAGE FOR REFERENCE INTERACTIONS
Ask before offering help.	Don't assume you know what the person wants. Making sure you understand what people want will ensure they feel heard and give them the opportunity to clarify.	"It sounds as if you want to learn how to find a peer-reviewed article in your discipline, is that right?"
Listen to understand emotions and needs.	Particularly when people are upset, it is easy to make assumptions about what they are experiencing and why.	"Are you feeling frustrated because you need to trust that you'll be able to print out your work before class?"
Paraphrase and reflect back what you hear.	This is a way to check your own understanding of what the other person is experiencing.	"I hear you expressing annoyance that the catalog interface is changed. Am I understanding that right?"

instructors who give contradictory instructions for assignments—on the contrary, the reference librarian can help students work out how to go to their professor and ask for clarification in an appropriate way.

Some of the strategies recommended in previous chapters will also support learners in developing their identity. For example, the peer-based reference model discussed in chapter 4 provides support to all the students involved. The peer leader demonstrates to another student, and training for peer reference mentors can be designed to include coaching and critical reflection, providing students with the benefits of trusted adults and the powerful interactions between the staff/faculty and students.

In summary, some reference strategies that support learners as they move through the seven vectors of identity development include

- acknowledging and naming learners' growth through emotional experiences; and
- giving learners an opportunity to help others.

Library Instruction and Identity Development

Teaching provides opportunities to incorporate identity development directly into learning. One way to do this is by giving students meaningful opportunities to make their own choices. This may mean giving them options for how to move through course material, or places where they can truly choose the subject they wish to inquire into.

Librarians can also consider ways to highlight materials that will challenge students' beliefs or support their identities. For example, when teaching about controlled vocabularies, you might note the Library of Congress Subject Headings representing materials about homosexuality have changed over time. Introducing points that connect with students' interests, and potentially with issues of identity, may not start a powerful conversation in the moment but can be one more potential point of entry for reflection and growth.

Finally, consider incorporating critical reflection into your teaching. Reflective activities can be used for dual purposes, to assess student learning while also giving students a chance to process and grow. Kelly Wooten, at Duke University, often uses a minute paper asking learners to share something they've learned, a question they still have, and how they feel after a one-shot in the archives (Kelly Wooten, personal communication, November 19, 2016). This helps students practice recognizing and sharing their emotions, while also collecting some information related to any affective learning outcomes, or barriers to learning.

In summary, some ways that instruction can support identity development include

- creating meaningful opportunities for choice in learning; and
- incorporating reflection throughout learning.

Library Outreach and Identity Development

In some ways, library outreach may be the most natural place to boost and support students in the process of identity development. As noted in previous chapters, outreach activities offer a less formal arena to interact with learners and can support learning for students at very different paces. In terms of identity development, outreach can offer serendipitous extracurricular engagement.

One of the most powerful ways that library outreach can connect with learners is through passive programs, such as displays and reading recommendations. Thoughtfully selected materials can connect to learners across a multiple of the seven vectors. For example, a thoughtfully selected display of books to support Native American Heritage Month (November) may celebrate some students' indigenous heritage, challenge other students to reconsider the impact of settler-colonialism, and reinforce an enjoyment of poetry in other students. However, a passive display becomes more meaningful still when it offers an opportunity for engagement, such as inviting passersby to share their own reflections and thoughts on a whiteboard.

Librarians can also connect with partners outside the library. One of the key influences that Chickering and Reisser identify is institutional objectives and how clearly the values are communicated across campus. In some ways, we can see this as the institutional equivalent to developing integrity, specifically congruence between beliefs and behaviors. The library can participate in campus-wide campaigns where appropriate, or simply collaborate with other units to reinforce messages. Incorporating students into programming gives students voice and can reinforce numerous vectors. See an example of how students can be involved in programming in the Generation Open box.

> **GENERATION OPEN AT THE UNIVERSITY OF ALBERTA**
>
> One way to give students a role in programming or event planning is to work with a particular course. In 2014, University of Alberta librarians Sarah Polkinghorne and Denise Koufogiannakis worked with faculty members and students in a design course to develop an exhibition of student art based on the Open Access Week theme "Generation Open" (Damon-Moore 2014). A close relationship with faculty ensured that the project both met the library's needs and created a meaningful learning experience for students, modeling the process that they hope to do in their careers as designers.

In summary, some outreach strategies that support identity development in learners include

- creating low-barrier opportunities to interact with engaging and challenging materials; and
- collaborating with outside partners to reinforce messages across an institution.

Key Points

Identity development can be a lifelong process, and each learner proceeds along a unique path. Understanding the elements of identity development can shape reference services, instruction, and outreach. Here are some key points to take away:

- One's sense of self becomes increasingly complex, and identity develops in conjunction with the people and the environment around us.

- Reference interactions can provide a time to help learners recognize their own growth by naming competences and acknowledging emotional experiences. Peer reference models also give learners a chance to learn from one another.
- Instruction can be shaped to support and challenge learners by providing meaningful opportunities for choice and by incorporating reflection throughout.
- Outreach activities can support learners at all stages of identity development, by providing opportunities to interact with challenging materials and through collaborations outside the library.

This chapter explored the value of using Chickering and Reisser's seven vectors of student identity development in your work as a librarian. Chapter 7 will build on these identity theories that help explain students' evolving sense of self and will examine how students engage with the learning experience. Chapter 7 will also describe opportunities that institutions can provide for engaging learners that are proven to positively influence student success.

References

American College Health Association. 2015. "American College Health Association National College Health Assessment II: Undergraduate Reference Group Executive Summary." http://www.acha-ncha.org/.

Association of American Colleges and Universities (AAC&U). 2014. "Essential Learning Outcomes." AAC&U, April 18. http://www.aacu.org/.

Chickering, A. W., and Linda Reisser. 1993. *Education and Identity*. 2nd ed. San Francisco: Jossey-Bass.

Crenshaw, Kimberle. 1989. "Demarginalizing the Intersection of Race and Sex: A Black Feminist Critique of Antidiscrimination Doctrine, Feminist Theory and Antiracist Politics." *University of Chicago Legal Forum*, p. 139.

Damon-Moore, Laura. 2014. "'Open Generation' Exhibition at Rutherford Library." Library as Incubator Project, December 3. http://www.libraryasincubatorproject.org/.

Erikson, Erik H. 1963. *Childhood and Society*. Rev. ed. 2nd ed. New York: Norton.

Evans, Nancy J., Deanna S. Forney, Florence M. Guido, Lori D. Patton, and Kristen A. Renn. 2010. *Student Development in College: Theory, Research, and Practice*. 2nd ed. Jossey-Bass Higher and Adult Education Series. San Francisco: Jossey-Bass.

Gross, Melissa, and Don Latham. 2007. "Attaining Information Literacy: An Investigation of the Relationship between Skill Level, Self-Estimates of Skill, and Library Anxiety." *Library and Information Science Research* 29 (3): 332–53.

Jiao, Qun G., Anthony J. Onwuegbuzie, and Art A. Lichtenstein. 1996. "Library Anxiety: Characteristics of 'at-Risk' College Students." *Library and Information Science Research* 18 (2): 151–63. doi:10.1016/S0740-8188(96)90017-1.

Kahn, Michael. 2002. *Basic Freud: Psychoanalytic Thought for the Twenty First Century*. New York: Basic Books.

Kwon, Nahyun, Anthony J. Onwuegbuzie, and Linda Alexander. 2007. "Critical Thinking Disposition and Library Anxiety: Affective Domains on the Space of Information Seeking and Use in Academic Libraries." *College and Research Libraries* 68 (3): 268–78. doi:10.5860/crl.68.3.268.

Miller, William R., and Stephen Rollnick. 2002. *Motivational Interviewing: Preparing People for Change*. 2nd ed. New York: Guilford Press.

Pascarella, Ernest T., and Patrick T. Terenzini. 2005. *How College Affects Students*. 2nd ed. San Francisco: Jossey-Bass.

Rosenberg, Marshall. 2003. *Nonviolent Communication: A Language of Life; Life-Changing Tools for Healthy Relationships*. Encinitas, CA: PuddleDancer.

Torres, Vasti, Susan R. Jones, and Kristen A. Renn. 2009. "Identity Development Theories in Student Affairs: Origins, Current Status, and New Approaches." *Journal of College Student Development* 50 (6): 577–96.

CHAPTER 7

Engaging Learners in Their Education

IN THIS CHAPTER

▷ Understanding what engagement means for learners

▷ Discussing the role of the library and staff in engaging learners

---

AS LEARNERS MOVE THROUGH the education system, their interest in classes, subjects, friends, and extracurricular activities goes through highs and lows. You can probably remember mornings when you did not want to go to school or evenings where you couldn't wait for the next day's activity. Learners are most successful when they are highly interested and engaged in their education. How can libraries and librarians help engage students in this way? Research into learner engagement over the past forty years can help librarians answer this question.

The topic of engagement was chosen for this chapter because of the popularity of the term "student engagement" at all levels of education in the United States. Student engagement refers to how learners become involved in all aspects of their education. Some of the factors of engagement are internal and vary with the individual learner. Other factors are external and can be shaped by the learner's environment. Librarians play a role in creating a more engaging learning environment in a range of settings from public to school and academic libraries. This chapter will delve further into the factors that influence learners' engagement and how librarians can systematically engage students in their learning.

Librarians connect with learners every day, in ways that are familiar to the general public: answering questions at reference desks, checking out books, and recommending leisure reading. In addition to these common modes of connection, librarians and libraries also work with learners in less visible ways. For example, in the course of a day, a librarian may have an impactful conversation with a student employee or volunteer, help design a study space that facilitates learner interaction, or host a book club in the library.

This chapter will cover student engagement, beginning with a brief historical overview including theoretical underpinnings such as Student Involvement Theory, and concluding with practical examples that are currently used at public, academic, and school libraries to engage students with their learning.

To better understand the concept and application of student engagement, it is important to recognize that research and the practical application of "student engagement" have developed along two separate pathways: one for higher education and one for K–12. (K–12 is a term used in the United States to describe everything before college and university.) This division is unfortunate but not surprising. The reason for the difference between the two understandings of student engagement is simple, although frustrating for practitioners: in the United States there is a communication gap between K–12 and higher education. The gap exists not just between K–12 teachers and university or college faculty but also between administrators of the two educational systems, and ultimately this chasm extends to the way research into these two educational systems is carried out. Therefore, the history and development of "student engagement" will be discussed as two separate pathways in this chapter, but an attempt will be made to bridge the gap by pointing out practical applications that may benefit learners at all levels of education.

Student Involvement Theory in Higher Education

The now popular term "student engagement" evolved out of the Student Involvement Theory developed by Alexander Astin (1984). As with many other student development theory creators, Astin concentrated all of his research on undergraduate students. An explanation of how this theory morphed into the current understanding of student engagement can help librarians contribute to students' decisions that ultimately affect their ability to stay in school and persist to graduation.

Astin founded the Higher Education Research Institute at UCLA and has been a leader in higher education for over fifty years; he continues his work as a professor emeritus at UCLA (Harmon 2016). In 1966 Astin began conducting a benchmark survey of freshmen university students (eventually seniors were included) and continued the survey annually for approximately five decades, concluding in 2014 (Pace and Kuh 2014). This survey charted characteristics and experiences of incoming students across the nation, and its results often made national news headlines (Mills 1999). With a background in developmental psychology, Astin was interested in learning how universities produced successful students and citizens (Mills 1999). He chose to survey students because he said, "to me, the test of anything in academia is how the students are affected, and I don't think we ought to be making policy in education in any other way. That ought to be the true test, the bottom line, the students' benefit. Is their development enhanced by this?" (Mills 1999, 2).

The survey instrument Astin developed was called the College Student Experiences Questionnaire (CSEQ), and it was designed to "learn something about how students are affected by different kinds of experiences in college" (Harmon 2016). One of the ways that colleges and universities used the results was to assess student involvement (Pace and Kuh 2014). Astin has said that "student involvement refers to the amount of physical and psychological energy that the student devotes to the academic experience" (Astin 1984, 518). For example, a university student who is highly involved may live in an on-campus residence hall, spend considerable time studying in the library, and be employed part time at the university bookstore. A student who is not very involved may routinely skip classes, avoid interacting with classmates and the faculty, and steer clear of the library, spending little to no time on campus outside of class. These are just examples, and of course there are many ways a student may be involved or uninvolved. The involvement of a sorority member studying business in Iowa may look very different from a student living in the residence halls in Florida and studying oceanography, but both students may be highly involved in their respective locations.

Astin developed the theory because he noticed a gap in the faculty and administrators' understanding of students (Astin 1984). As he described it in an interview in 1984,

> A major impetus for the development of the student involvement theory was my exasperation at the tendency of many academics to treat the student as a "black box." On the input end of this black box are the various policies and programs of a college or university; on the output end are various types of achievement measures such as GPA or scores on standardized tests." (Astin 1984: 519)

The student involvement theory provides a substitute for the missing "black box." Astin (1984) began developing the theory after conducting a longitudinal study on college dropouts as he attempted to identify the factors that affected student persistence to graduation. Using the idea of involvement, Astin found the factors that contributed to persistence suggested involvement and the factors that contributed to dropping out suggested a lack of involvement. The theory of student involvement was validated through the annual administration of the CSEQ to university freshman and seniors. The five principles of student involvement are described in the box below.

THE FIVE BASIC PRINCIPLES OF STUDENT INVOLVEMENT THEORY

1. Involvement refers to the amount of physical and psychological energy students put into various activities.
2. Involvement occurs along a continuum; a student's involvement can be high or low at various times in different activities.
3. Involvement has both quantitative and qualitative features.
4. The amount of learning and personal development related to any program is proportional to the quality and quantity of student involvement in that program.
5. The effectiveness of any policy or practice is directly related to the capacity of that policy or practice to increase student involvement. (Astin 1984, 519)

Student Engagement Application in Higher Education

In 2014, the CSEQ was discontinued as a nationwide instrument, in part because the National Survey of Student Engagement (NSSE) had usurped it within higher education. The NSSE was developed as an initiative of the Pew Charitable Trusts beginning with a group that was convened in 1998 to discuss measurements of quality in higher education and college ranking systems in the United States, such as the *U.S. News and*

World Report (Center for Postsecondary Research 2001). The NSSE was established with the intention of offering a new tool to gather information about higher education quality to share and use in local and national conversations; many of the questions on the NSSE were derived from other existing student questionnaires, including the CSEQ. The NSSE had a broader scope than the CSEQ and has several purposes including improving undergraduate education, providing data and information to accreditation bodies, and helping prospective students choose their university or college based on overall quality. Like the CSEQ the NSSE is also administered during the freshmen and senior years, to students who have attended their college or university for at least two terms, in order to capture student experience during two points in their academics and paint a fairer picture of that institution. The team that developed the NSSE included several leaders in the study of higher education, including Alexander Astin. Today the NSSE is widely used; in 2016, it was administered to 537 U.S. and Canadian institutions, receiving 311,086 responses from students in their first and senior years (Center for Postsecondary Research 2016).

Student Engagement Defined

As the NSSE overtook the CSEQ, the use of the term "student engagement" also overtook the term "student involvement." Although they are often used interchangeably in the research literature and in higher education, student engagement currently appears to be the more popular term (see figure 7.1).

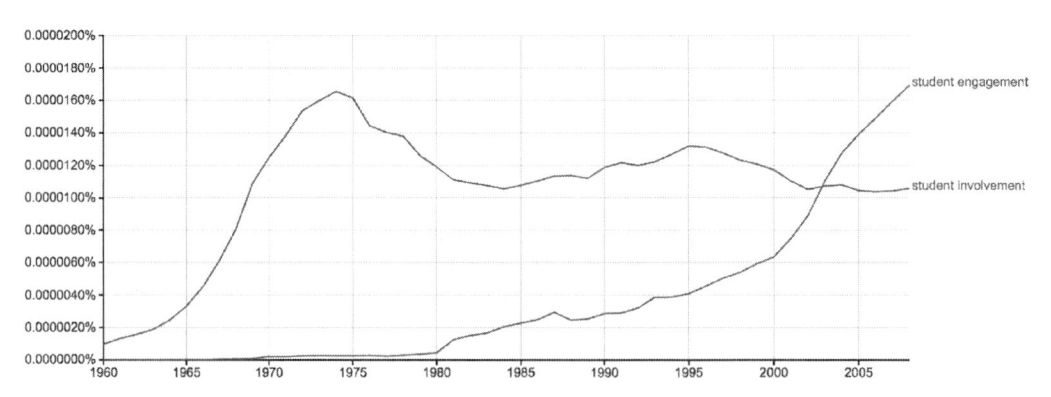

Figure 7.1. Google Books Ngram Viewer: frequency of the phrases "student engagement" and "student involvement" in a corpus of books over the selected years 1960–2008

As mentioned in chapter 1, student development theories are often ill defined. A report about student engagement from the Higher Education Academy in the UK, written by Vicki Trowler (2010), notes that many papers and conference proceedings about student engagement do not contain a definition of the term "student engagement," leading to the false assumption that a definition is universally shared. Research and practical application are somewhat confusing due to this lack of a shared definition; therefore, in the box below you will find Trowler's definition, which will be used for the purpose of this chapter.

STUDENT ENGAGEMENT DEFINITION

"Student engagement is concerned with the interaction between the time, effort, and other relevant resources invested by both students and their institutions intended to optimize the student experience and enhance the learning outcomes and development of students and the performance, and reputation of the institution" (Trowler 2010, 2).

Student Engagement and Libraries

The NSSE does not include questions about the library or library services (although optional questions can be added by individual institutions); however, there is much to be learned by library staff from the data gathered from the NSSE and subsequent articles and research. See the box below for example questions from the NSSE.

SAMPLE QUESTIONS FROM THE 2016 NATIONAL SURVEY OF STUDENT ENGAGEMENT (NSSE)

During the current school year, how often have you done the following? (*very often*, *often*, *sometimes*, or *never*)

- Talked about career plans with a faculty member
- Worked with a faculty member on activities other than coursework (committees, student groups, etc.)
- Discussed course topics, ideas, or concepts with a faculty member outside of class
- Discussed your academic performance with a faculty member

During the current school year, how much has your coursework emphasized the following? (*very much*, *quite a bit*, *some*, or *very little*)

- Analyzing an idea, experience, or line of reasoning in depth by examining its parts
- Evaluating a point of view, decision, or information source
- Forming a new idea or understanding from various pieces of information (NSSE 2016)

As universities and colleges embrace the NSSE and discuss the results, what can libraries, librarians, and library staff do to increase student engagement? The justification for increasing student engagement aligns with academic institutions' larger mission of increasing retention and raising student achievement. But this may be a shift in thinking and practice for many librarians, because historically libraries have shown their value through quantitative measures related to collections. For example, ARL (Association of Research Libraries) membership in the United States is focused on collections, acquisition, and staff and requires members to provide statistical indicators each year including number of volumes held, number of current serial titles received, total library expenditures, and total salaries. In 1998, a similar focus on resource and process measures within higher education led the Pew Charitable Trusts to convene a working group that ultimately resulted in the development of the NSSE (Center for Postsecondary Research 2001). Therefore, the tendency to count things, such as books, students, employees, and so forth, is not unique to librarians. Measuring and reporting how libraries increase student engagement can only benefit libraries and students. Many librarians already incorporate practices that are shown to engage students and lead to persistence to graduation and higher achievement. More examples for including these practices in the work librarians do will be discussed later in the chapter.

Student Engagement and High-Impact Practices

It's important to note that although "student engagement" focuses on the *student*, one of the most important aspects of student engagement is how the institution uses resources and learning opportunities to engage learners. One publication that uses the data from the NSSE is George Kuh's "High-Impact Educational Practices" report, which was funded by the Association of American Colleges and Universities (AAC&U) and can be used by librarians to identify how their library can employ high-impact practices to increase student engagement. According to the report, in order to achieve the learning outcomes that both educators and future employers endorse, institutions must connect these outcomes with student engagement through a "thoughtfully planned sequence of high-impact practices" (Kuh 2008, 8). Research has shown a relationship between these high-impact practices and increased student retention and achievement (Kuh 2008). Libraries and librarians can use these proven practices to develop new programs and services and then turn around and show stakeholders, such as students, upper administration, and parents, that they are implementing these practices.

HIGH-IMPACT PRACTICES IDENTIFIED BY THE AAC&U

- First-year seminars and experiences
- Common intellectual experiences
- Learning communities
- Writing intensive courses
- Collaborative assignments and projects
- Diversity/global learning
- Undergraduate research
- Service learning, community-based learning
- Internships
- Capstone projects and courses (Kuh 2008, 9–11)

Kuh suggests that institutions take action to ensure that every student participates in at least two of the practices in order to create "purposeful pathways" to move students through the learning they need for a successful future (Kuh 2008, 7). The next section will further explore three high-impact practices and practical applications in libraries.

Instruction and the High-Impact Practice of First-year Seminars and Experiences

As mentioned earlier, Kuh (2008) suggested that every undergraduate student participate in two high-impact practices (HIPs), but he also emphasized that one of those activities should be in the student's first year. There is a multitude of ways, including instruction, that librarians can engage with students during this critical time; in fact, librarians have been an integral part of first-year efforts since they began in the 1970s (Gilbert et al. 1997).

Teaching a first-year semester or term-long course is one way librarians can provide information literacy instruction during the first year and support their institution's efforts to increase retention. At the University of Tennessee, Knoxville (UTK), several librarians have taught thematic freshmen seminar courses, intended to help students in the academic and social transition to the university. Instructors choose a topic they are passionate about and develop and deliver the curriculum; UTKs topics have included Mardi Gras and the World's Fair. Through these classes the librarians not only teach about information literacy but also stay connected with undergraduates as unofficial mentors after their class has concluded (Braquet and Westfall 2011).

The University of Toronto at Scarborough (UTSC) librarians offer a popular summer workshop before students take their first class at the university. Titled the Summer Learning Institute (SLI) in Research, Writing, and Presenting, this two-day intensive workshop is coordinated by two librarians and helps students in the transition from high school to their first year at the university. In 2006, the enrollment in this noncredit course was 280 students divided into eight classes of 35 students each, and reviews were overwhelmingly positive. The librarians that facilitate the program say that it accomplishes its intended information literacy goals and actively engages students while easing them into their new university (Guise et al. 2008).

Reference and the High-Impact Practice of Collaborative Assignments and Projects

This HIP combines two goals: for learners to work with others to solve problems and for learners to listen to the insights of others in order to increase their own understanding (Kuh 2008). Student employees, by nature of their roles in the library, work on collaborative assignments and projects. Libraries can take a systematic approach to facilitate learning by framing student positions to maximize opportunities and prepare learners for future employment after graduation. At the University of Wisconsin, Eau Claire, the library incorporated elements of HIPs in their students' work experience (Markgraf 2015). For example, they now use the student interview process as a teachable moment, recognizing that it may be one of the only opportunities students have to practice interviewing before entering the professional job market. Therefore, they treat every interview as a professional interview by requesting résumés and references, asking "real" questions, and providing feedback after the interview process. In addition, they added in annual reviews and created opportunities for self-reflection on the work experience.

Encouraging interactions at the reference desk between librarians and student employees is a simple way to purposefully create opportunities for learners to engage with and learn from coworkers who have different life experiences and backgrounds; in addition, increasing these interactions may lead to informal or formal mentoring. Robert Reason, Patrick Terenzini, and Robert Domingo (2006) suggest that improving relationships between students and faculty members may be effective at increasing students' perceptions of a supportive campus environment.

Reference librarians can work with students to identify new ways that underutilized space can be used. Redesigning library space for group work is one way to encourage collaboration. Some libraries have purposely created presentation practice rooms so that students can practice individual or group presentations. The University of California San Diego's practice rooms are equipped with a projector, computer, keyboard, and lectern. Students are encouraged to check out a video camera for instant feedback (The Library 2016).

Outreach and the High-Impact Practice: Diversity/Global Learning

This HIP addresses the need for global competencies. In a 2007 AAC&U survey, 46 percent of employers said that recent college graduates are "not well prepared" with global knowledge (Kuh 2008, 5). Gary Pike and George Kuh (2005) suggest that merely increasing diversity and interaction among diverse groups is not enough; instead, institutions need to foster group equality and intergroup collaboration as well as opportunities for people of diverse groups to get to know one another. Libraries can take an active role in facilitating cross-cultural interactions in their libraries. Facilitating positive interactions between groups may increase positive perceptions of the interpersonal environment within institutions (Pike and Kuh 2005).

Several libraries have implemented international speed friending, an activity that is described in detail in chapter 6. This informal event, housed in the library, encourages interaction between international and domestic learners or language learners. There are at least three libraries currently hosting speed-friending events: Oregon State University, University of Colorado, and Heights Branch Public Library in Texas. Beginning a speed-friending event starts by identifying a partner. For example, the library at Oregon State University partners with their English-language learning program.

Another activity that addresses diversity/global learning is study abroad. Librarians might be surprised to learn that the most popular form of study abroad in the United States is currently short-term, faculty-led courses. Librarians at universities may be eligible to lead study abroad. At Oregon State University (OSU), two librarians, Laurie Bridges and Kelly McElroy, created a librarian-led study abroad; the first three-credit class took place in the summer of 2016, and each summer two librarians at OSU plan to take a group of undergraduate students abroad for a short, immersive, experiential-learning course titled "Information and Global Social Justice." By reaching out to campus organizations that served underrepresented students, the librarians were able to make new and valuable connections for the library while also attracting students who fell into at least one of three groups: students of color, Pell Grant eligible, and first-generation college students. As Kuh (2008) notes, study abroad can be life changing and deepens learning, providing perspective to students about themselves and their place in the larger world.

California State University, Fresno, partners with their international student services and programs to host a weekly "International Coffee Hour" delivered by international students in the library. Every week during the academic year, students give presentations about their hometown, country, and culture. The event is open to the public and usually attracts fifty to sixty people per program (Pun 2016).

Student Engagement in Primary/Secondary School

Up until this point in the chapter, the scholarly research and discussion about student engagement has focused on higher education. The next section will focus primarily on student engagement in primary and secondary school, referred to as K–12 in the United States. As discussed previously in this chapter, the understanding of student engagement in higher education environments evolved out of Alexander Astin's work in the 1960s; however, in K–12 the discussion began in the 1980s in relation to high school student dropout and completion rates (Reschly and Christenson 2012). The remainder of this section will consider student engagement as it relates to current understanding in the K–12 school system.

As in higher education, student engagement in K–12 literature is not well defined. In their preface to the *Handbook of Research on Student Engagement*, the editors note that there is an abundance of definitions that differ based on how educators think about student outcomes, what motivates students to be engaged, and the role schools play in encouraging these behaviors (Christenson, Reschly, and Wylie 2012). The purpose of their handbook is to address the "unknowns" of the research and theory of student engagement, and each chapter author was asked to define engagement based on their experiences. Despite these "unknowns," the editors do emphasize that engagement is particularly important for students who are at high risk for dropping out of school and that engagement benefits all students.

Although student engagement in K–12 does not have a single definition, researchers in this area have looked at various aspects and produced suggestions for teachers that can easily be used by librarians to increase learners' engagement with their education. For example, resilience research into engagement focuses on how students respond to setbacks and difficulties in school; by modeling resilient behaviors, such as admitting mistakes and sharing stories of educational difficulties, librarians can model "constructive coping" (Skinner and Pitzer 2012, 32). This is something that librarians do daily during reference interviews. The next sections will look at different aspects of engagement for children and teenagers and include suggestions for librarian practice.

Engagement and Students of Color

In the United States, the public education system has been designed by the majority white culture; in addition, 82 percent of teachers in the system are white (Policy and Program Studies Service, 2016). The trend in U.S. libraries is similar: 87 percent of librarians are white. However, students in the public education system are predominantly persons of color (Policy and Program Studies Service 2016). This disparity, coupled with the underachievement of African American, Latino, and Native American students, has led to research on how engagement may explain the variation in achievement between ethnic groups. One of the many possible factors that may contribute to a lack of engagement by students of color is the structure of the institution and how it may support or inhibit their engagement.

First, although research is limited, studies have shown a correlation between the ethnicity of educators in schools and student engagement. When historically minoritized students are in schools with higher percentages of minority educators, there is a positive correlation with engagement (Bingham and Okagaki 2012). A solution libraries can implement to increase learner engagement for students of color would be to diversify the librarian profession, but this shift in staffing will not happen rapidly. A quicker option for increasing diversity is to carefully consider the diversity of the student aides, staff members, and volunteers in your library. Encouraging students from underrepresented groups to work as a librarian aid may pique a child's interest in librarianship and eventually add to the pipeline of those drawn to the library profession, thereby leading to equitable representation of librarians of color.

Second, relationships between an educator and learner may provide the support the learner needs to navigate differences between home and school environments, deal with discrimination and failure, and promote a positive attitude about learning and education (Bingham and Okagaki 2012). A supportive educator is one who listens to, encourages, and respects students. Supportive relationships between educators and learners have been shown to have a positive correlation between behavior and emotional engagement for students from ethnic minorities (Bingham and Okagaki 2012). One simple way to show children and teenagers you are listening to them is to have a location in your library where they can use adhesive notes to recommend new book titles or subjects (see figure 7.2)—let them know you are listening by stamping the adhesive note with a library stamp (Marta Bondia, personal communication, June 29, 2016).

Engagement in Reading

Children and youth who are engaged with reading are motivated to read, comprehend, and construct meaning from what they are reading and interact socially about reading (Guthrie, Wigfield, and You 2012). An engagement framework depicting the direct and indirect effects of classroom practices on student reading outcomes has been developed by University of Maryland researchers John Guthrie, Allan Wigfield, and Wei You (see figure 7.3). The framework represents reading engagement processes that are motivational, behavioral, and cognitive. Guthrie, Wigfield, and You (2012) indicate that classroom practices, shown on the far left side of the diagram, have both direct and indirect effects on competence, shown to the right side of the diagram, which are mediated by motivations and behavior management. The researchers have highlighted practices that impact student motivations in the classroom; in K–12 schools, the library is routinely used as a classroom space by librarians and teachers.

One classroom practice found to impact student motivation is autonomy support (Guthrie, Wigfield, and You 2012). Librarians support autonomy in the library daily by providing free-choice learning opportunities, for example, students choosing their own books and librarians giving reader's advisories that consider student feelings and perspectives. Students who are given autonomy support have been shown to place a higher value on reading, and not surprisingly, research has found middle school students who are given little or no choice about what they are reading in language arts or science classes show a loss in intrinsic motivation for reading (Guthrie, Mason-Singh, and Coddington 2012).

In addition, incorporating relevance into autonomy support increases the value of reading in the classroom; for example, explaining why students are reading a particular textbook, and how it may help them in the future, increases students' valuing of those

Figure 7.2. Recommendation area for the youth section at Biblioteca Sagrada Família in Barcelona, Catalonia, Spain

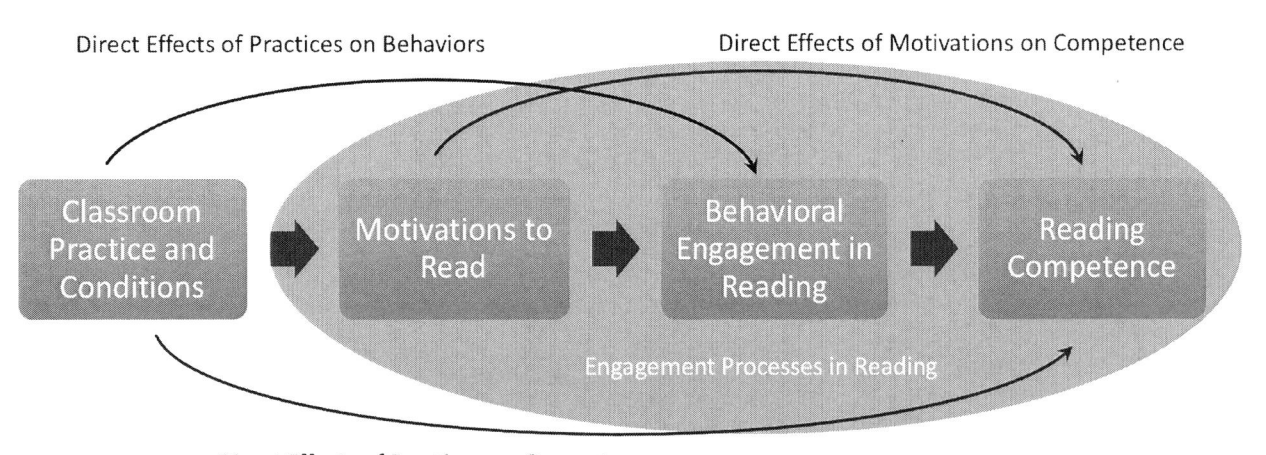

Direct Effects of Practices on Behaviors   Direct Effects of Motivations on Competence

Classroom Practice and Conditions → Motivations to Read → Behavioral Engagement in Reading → Reading Competence

Engagement Processes in Reading

Direct Effects of Practices on Competence

Figure 7.3. Engagement processes in reading framework. *Developed by Guthrie, Wigfield, and You (2012).*

texts (Guthrie, Mason-Singh, and Coddington 2012). Librarians may boost learner interest in their classrooms by providing students with books that relate to what they are learning in class and pointing out how what they are learning might relate to their future careers. For an example, see the box below.

> **READING RELEVANCE, FREE-CHOICE LEARNING, AND ENGAGEMENT**
>
> In second grade at Garfield elementary school (Corvallis, Oregon), the students are learning about arthropods. The classroom teacher has taken the students to see the arthropod collection at the nearby university. The librarian can draw student attention to nonfiction books in the library about arthropods, their habitats, climate change, and science careers; the librarian can also highlight fiction books

Key Points

Learners are more successful when they are involved with their education. To this end, librarians can engage in various educational practices to increase learner engagement. Here are some key points to take away:

- Student Involvement Theory in higher education is the foundation on which the current understanding of "student engagement" is built.
- In higher education librarians can use high-impact practices (HIPs) as part of their institution's effort to increase retention and student achievement.
- Librarians at all levels of education can facilitate student engagement by focusing on interpersonal relationships with students.

Although there currently exists a gap between student engagement research and application between K–12 institutions and higher education, librarians can use what is currently known to facilitate the success of their learners. Chapter 8 will review the key points of the theories covered in this book to help you more easily make connections between theories.

References

Astin, Alexander. 1984. "Student Involvement: A Developmental Theory for Higher Education." *Journal of College Student Personnel* 25 (4): 518–29.

Bingham, Gary E., and Lynn Okagaki. 2012. "Ethnicity and Student Engagement." In *Handbook of Research on Student Engagement*, edited by Sandra L. Christenson, Amy L. Reschly, and Cathy Wylie, 65–95. New York: Springer.

Braquet, Donna, and Micheline Westfall. 2011. "Of Fairs and Festivals: Librarians Teach Thematic First-Year Seminars." *Southeastern Librarian* 59 (1): 3–8.

Center for Postsecondary Research. 2001. "About NSSE: Our Origins and Potential." National Survey of Student Engagement, Indiana University School of Education. http://nsse.indiana.edu/.

———. 2016. "NSSE 2016 Overview." National Survey of Student Engagement, Indiana University School of Education, July 28. http://nsse.indiana.edu/.

Christenson, Sandra L., Amy L. Reschly, and Cathy Wylie. 2012. "Preface." In *Handbook of Research on Student Engagement*, edited by Sandra L. Christenson, Amy L. Reschly, and Cathy Wylie, v–ix. New York: Springer.

Gilbert, Sid, Judy Chapman, Peter Dietsche, Paul Grayson, and John N. Gardner. 1997. "From Best Intentions to Best Practices: The First-Year Experience in Canadian Postsecondary Education." National Resource Center for the Freshman Year Experience and Students in Transition Monograph Series Number 22. http://eric.ed.gov/.

Guise, Janneka L., Janet Goosney, Shannon Gordon, and Heather J. Pretty. 2008. "Evolution of a Summer Research/Writing Workshop for First-Year University Students." *New Library World* 109 (5/6): 235–50.

Guthrie, John T., Amanda Mason-Singh, and Cassandra S. Coddington. 2012. "Instructional Effects of Concept-Oriented Reading Instruction on Motivation for Reading Information Text in Middle School." In *Adolescents' Engagement in Academic Literacy*, edited by John T. Guthrie, Allan Wigfield, and Susan Lutz Klauda, 155–215. College Park, MD: University of Maryland.

Guthrie, John T., Allan Wigfield, and Wei You. 2012. "Instructional Contexts for Engagement and Achievement in Reading." In *Handbook of Research on Student Engagement*, edited by Sandra L. Christenson, Amy L. Reschly, and Cathy Wylie, 601–34. New York: Springer.

Harmon, Joanie. 2016. "Alexander Astin Looks Back at 50 Years of 'The American Freshman.'" *Ampersand*, May 5. https://ampersand.gseis.ucla.edu/.

Kuh, George D. 2008. "High-Impact Educational Practices: What They Are, Who Has Access to Them, and Why They Matter." Association of American Colleges and Universities Leap Report, Washington, DC. http://provost.tufts.edu/.

The Library. 2016. "Presentation and Practice Rooms." University of California San Diego, July 28. http://libraries.ucsd.edu/.

Markgraf, Jill. 2015. "Unleash Your Library's HIPster: Transforming Student Library Jobs into High-Impact Practices." In ACRL 2015 Proceedings, Portland, OR, 770–77. http://www.ala.org/.

Mills, Kay. 1999. "Alexander Astin." *Los Angeles Times*, April 18. http://articles.latimes.com/.

NSSE (National Survey of Student Engagement). 2016. http://nsse.indiana.edu/pdf/survey_instruments/2016/NSSE_2016-US_English.pdf.

Pace, C. Robert, and George D. Kuh. 2014. "College Student Experiences Questionnaire (CSEQ) Assessment Program: General Info." Indiana University Center for the Study of Postsecondary Research, Bloomington. http://cseq.indiana.edu/.

Pike, Gary R., and George D. Kuh. 2005. "A Typology of Student Engagement for American Colleges and Universities." *Research in Higher Education* 46 (2): 185–209.

Policy and Program Studies Service. 2016. "The State of Racial Diversity in the Educator Workforce." Office of Planning, Evaluation and Policy Development, U.S. Department of Education, July. https://www2.ed.gov/.

Pun, Ray. 2016. "The Library Diversity Committee: Supporting Diversity and Inclusivity in the Academic Community." WebJunction, September 15. http://www.webjunction.org/.

Reason, Robert, Patrick Terenzini, and Robert Domingo. 2006. "First Things First: Developing Academic Competence in the First Year of College." *Research in Higher Education* 47 (2): 149–75.

Reschly, Amy L., and Christenson, Sandra L. 2012. "Jingle, Jangle, and Conceptual Haziness: Evolution and Future Directions of the Engagement Construct." In *Handbook of Research on*

Student Engagement, edited by Sandra L. Christenson, Amy L. Reschly, and Cathy Wylie, 3–19. New York: Springer.

Skinner, Ellen A., and Jennifer R. Pitzer. 2012. "Developmental Dynamics of Student Engagement, Coping, and Everyday Resilience." In *Handbook of Research on Student Engagement*, edited by Sandra L. Christenson, Amy L. Reschly, and Cathy Wylie, 21–45. New York: Springer.

Trowler, Vicki. 2010. "Student Engagement Literature Review." Higher Education Academy report, Lancaster University, York, UK, November. http://www.lancaster.ac.uk/.

CHAPTER 8

Connecting Current and Future Theories

IN THIS CHAPTER

▷ Reviewing development theories for integration into practice

▷ Discussing future directions for new theories to explore

▷ Collecting feedback as a way to regularly reflect on your practice

---

THEORIES ARE VALUABLE TOOLS FOR LIBRARIANS who wish to develop a reflective, empathetic approach to their work. This book has focused on a particular subset of theories—student development theories. Throughout this book, you have seen examples of the different contexts in which these development theories can be applied. You have also learned that while theories can synthesize a broader set of experiences into a framework that defines and explains behaviors, theories must also be modified based on societal and cultural changes. One of the most important societal shifts that has occurred in recent decades is an increasing awareness that the experiences of a single homogeneous group cannot represent a standard that all other groups must adapt to or be measured against. Paying attention to your learners' needs and actively engaging them as you try out new reference, instruction, or outreach activities will help you maintain balance and flexibility in the way theory informs your practice.

This book focused on three main student development theory areas: cognitive and intellectual, identity, and engagement theories. These theories were chosen because of their long-standing importance and use in the student affairs field and because of their relevance to libraries. However, there are other student development theories that were not covered in this book. Those theories include moral development theory, which focuses on understandings of right and wrong, as well as personality type theories and learning-style theories. While those theories have previously informed the work of student affairs personnel, they are currently not used as much or are not as applicable to the library context. Hopefully the theories discussed provided you with some opportunities for reflection about how you interact with learners in your specific context and have whetted your appetite for exploring more theories.

Theories are constantly changing. This last chapter will begin with a brief review of some of the main takeaways from the theories covered. This chapter will also suggest some future directions for student development theories, especially in light of changes that may affect libraries. In addition, some approaches for assessing the use of theories, for crafting guiding statements, and for building connections with relevant partners will be discussed to provide some final options for incorporating theories into your practice.

Student Development Theory Key Takeaways

Cognitive and intellectual, identity, and engagement theories were discussed throughout this book. As noted in chapter 1, theories addressing human behaviors are not meant to be used separately in a stand-alone manner. Human behavior is complex and influenced by a range of internal and external factors. As a result, an integrative approach to working with individuals that values their unique challenges and supports is recommended. The key points of each of the seven theories covered in this book are reviewed below and presented in table 8.1 to help you more easily see the connections between each of these theories. In addition, suggested library practices based on the student development theories are provided in table 8.2.

Intellectual and Ethical Development Theory

Perry's Intellectual and Ethical Development Theory led the way for student affairs professionals and other college student services providers to begin recognizing the way learners' ability to deal with new information inside and outside of the classroom changed over time. William Perry proposed three major stages—*dualism*, *multiplicity*, and *relativism*—to delineate typical intellectual development steps. Perry argued that learners encountered transition points that influenced how and when learners shift to a new stage. The following key points and practices summarize the Intellectual and Ethical Development Theory:

- Learners absorb and make meaning in different ways when faced with new information depending on their intellectual and ethical development stage.
- Intellectual development problems emphasize understanding where sources of authority come from and how evidence is evaluated.
- Practitioners should recognize differences between the stages and look for ways to provide growth opportunities.

Key practices for librarians based on Perry's Intellectual and Ethical Development Theory include

- using a scaffolded system to introduce conversations about authority to learners at different developmental stages;
- providing opportunities for reflection on learning experiences; and
- establishing the library as a safe space for asking questions.

Table 8.1. Summary of student development theories

THEORY AREAS	THEORIES DISCUSSED	KEY POINTS OF THE THEORY	STAGES OF THE THEORY
Cognitive and intellectual	Intellectual and Ethical Development Theory[1]	• Faced with new information, learners absorb and make meaning in different ways depending on their intellectual and ethical development stage. • Emphasis on authority and evidence • Focus on traditional, college-aged learners • Key practices include recognizing differences between stages and providing growth opportunities.	• Dualism • Multiplicity • Relativism
	Reflective Judgment Model[2]	• Explains how learners deal with "ill-structured problems" at different intellectual development stages • Addresses intellectual development challenges that extend beyond traditional, college-aged learners • Key practices include learning to ask deeper questions when faced with ill-structured and uncomfortable problems.	• Prereflective thinking • Quasi-reflective thinking • Reflective thinking
	Epistemological Reflection Model[3]	• Diverse background experiences influence the intellectual strategies learners use. • Maintaining a sense of internal perspective is an intellectual ability that develops over time. • Key practices include providing opportunities for reflection in a variety of ways.	• Absolute knowing • Transitional knowing • Independent knowing • Contextual knowing
	Learning Partnerships Model[4]	• Learners process and use new information to create their own ideas and voice—"self authoring." • Shifts from relying on experts as the primary source of knowledge to learning in partnership with educators • Key practices include encouraging learners to build on their personal experiences to develop their own internal voice.	• Dependence • Independence • Interdependence
Identity	Identity Development Theory[5]	• Identity development is not always linear. • Establishing identity is the overarching outcome of all of the vectors. • Key practices include acknowledging and naming learners' emotional growth experiences and providing meaningful opportunities for choice.	• Developing competence • Managing emotions • Moving through autonomy toward interdependence • Developing mature interpersonal relationships • Establishing identity • Developing purpose • Developing integrity
Engagement	Student Involvement Theory[6]	• Learners are impacted by different experiences in school or college, which can affect their level of engagement. • The amount of physical and psychological energy learners give to the academic experience may be linked to persistence. • Key practices include incorporating high-impact practices known to increase learner engagement.	• Not based on stages

Notes
1. Perry 1970.
2. King and Kitchener 1994.
3. Baxter Magolda 1992.
4. Baxter Magolda 2008.
5. Chickering and Reisser 1993.
6. Astin 1984.

Table 8.2. Summary of suggested library practices based on student development theories

THEORY AREAS	THEORIES DISCUSSED	LIBRARY PRACTICES
Cognitive and intellectual	Intellectual and Ethical Development Theory	• Use a scaffolded system to introduce conversations about authority to learners at different developmental stages. • Provide opportunities for reflection on learning experiences. • Establish the library as a safe space for asking questions.
	Reflective Judgment Model	• Model a variety of approaches for dealing with difficult questions. • Discuss the contextual nature of authority.
	Epistemological Reflection Model	• Work together with learners to solve problems. • Incorporate a range of private and public, and written and spoken, reflection techniques.
	Learning Partnerships Model	• Incorporate examples from learners' everyday experiences. • Connect learning to experiences outside of academia. • Provide spaces for voices from throughout your community to be shared.
Identity	Identity Development Theory	• Build in meaningful opportunities for choice in learning. • Create low-barrier opportunities to interact with engaging and challenging materials. • Collaborate with outside partners to reinforce messages across an institution.
Engagement	Student Involvement Theory	• Focus on learners at key transition points such as when they first begin college. • Give learners opportunities to work with and listen to others to solve problems. • Actively work to create a library workforce that better represents the diversity of the broader society.

Reflective Judgment Model

Patricia King and Karen Kitchener's Reflective Judgment Model (1994) expanded on the Intellectual and Ethical Development Theory by looking at how both traditionally aged college students and older learners faced difficult, uncomfortable problems without clear-cut answers. King and Kitchener also offer three stages—*prereflective thinking*, *quasi-reflective thinking*, and *reflective thinking*—to illustrate how learners deal with difficult questions as they develop new, reflective approaches. Learning to address difficult problems takes practice and doesn't happen overnight. The following key points and practices summarize the Reflective Judgment Model:

- Learners deal with "ill-structured problems" using varied strategies depending on their intellectual development stage.
- Learners don't stop facing intellectual development challenges after college but continue developing reflective judgment strategies throughout the life-span.
- Practitioners should facilitate learning experiences that encourage asking deeper questions when faced with ill-structured and uncomfortable problems.

Key practices for librarians based on the Reflective Judgment Model include

- modeling a variety of approaches for dealing with difficult questions; and
- discussing the contextual nature of authority.

Epistemological Reflection Model

Marcia Baxter Magolda's Epistemological Reflection Model (1992) also expanded on earlier intellectual development theories by recognizing that the way people face intellectual choices is informed by their unique background experiences. Cultural, gender, and racial norms all impact the way that people make sense of information, and all of these diverse experiences are valued. Baxter Magolda (1992) describes four developmental groupings: *absolute knowing*, *transitional knowing*, *independent knowing*, and *contextual knowing*. New ways of knowing are influenced by setting aside times for intentional reflection. The following key points and practices summarize the Epistemological Reflection Model:

- Diverse background experiences influence the intellectual strategies learners use and when they begin using them.
- Maintaining a sense of internal perspective is an intellectual ability that develops over time.
- Practitioners should provide a range of structured and unstructured reflective opportunities.

Key practices for librarians based on the Epistemological Reflection Model include

- working together with learners to solve problems; and
- incorporating a range of private and public, and written and spoken, reflection techniques.

Learning Partnerships Model

Baxter Magolda (2004) also proposed the Learning Partnerships Model as a way to support and challenge learners to become more comfortable with their own internal identities and ways of knowing as they develop strategies for seeking information in partnership with others. The Learning Partnerships Model does not suggest developmental stages; however, self-authoring abilities tend to follow a trajectory of relational *dependence* to *independence* to *interdependence*. Because of its emphasis on relationships, the Learning Partnerships Model is a bridge to theories about identity. The following key points and practices summarize the Learning Partnerships Model:

- Learners process and use new information to create their own ideas and voice—a state known as "self authoring."
- Learners shift from relying on experts as the primary source of knowledge to learning in partnership with educators.
- Practitioners should encourage learners to build on their personal experiences to develop their own internal voice.

Key practices for librarians based on the Learning Partnerships Model include

- incorporating examples from learners' everyday experiences;
- connecting learning to experiences outside of academia; and
- providing spaces for voices from throughout your community to be shared.

Identity Development Theory

Arthur Chickering, later joined by Linda Reisser (1993), was instrumental in describing how identity, or sense of self, changes and grows throughout the life-span. Chickering developed seven vectors that explore main areas of growth over time. The first four vectors—*developing competence, managing emotions, moving toward interdependence*, and *developing mature interpersonal relationships*—are the most foundational. The following key points and practices summarize the Identity Development Theory:

- Identity development is not always linear, and growth in the vector areas can overlap.
- Establishing identity is the overarching outcome of all of the vectors.
- Practitioners should acknowledge learners' emotional growth experiences and provide meaningful opportunities for choice in learning environments.

Key practices for librarians based on the Identity Development Theory include

- building in meaningful opportunities for choice in learning;
- creating low-barrier opportunities to interact with engaging and challenging materials; and
- collaborating with outside partners to reinforce messages across an institution.

Student Involvement Theory

Alexander Astin (1984) explored student behaviors to see how their involvement in a variety of activities inside and outside of school affected their success in school. Astin noted that some of the factors of involvement, now referred to more commonly as "engagement," are internal and vary with the individual learner. Other factors are external and can be shaped by the learner's environment. Overall Astin found that students who are more engaged are more successful. As a result, increased effort has been placed on providing opportunities and supports for students to be engaged. The following key points and practices summarize the Student Involvement Theory:

- Learners are impacted by different experiences in school or college, which can affect their level of engagement.
- The amount of physical and psychological energy learners give to the academic experience can be linked to persistence.
- Practitioners should incorporate high-impact practices known to increase learner engagement.

Key practices for librarians based on the Student Involvement Theory include

- focusing on learners at key transition points such as when they first begin college;
- giving learners opportunities to work with and listen to others to solve problems; and
- actively working to create a library workforce that better represents the diversity of the broader society.

Future Directions for Student Development Theories

Both researchers and practitioners continually reflect on the behaviors they observe in the populations they work with. These reflections and observations lead to shifts in the way theories are applied. Sometimes gaps in current theories are large enough that it is necessary to create new theories. An overarching issue in student development theories is the tension between using broad theories to describe behaviors and the acknowledgment that many, substantial differences exist between groups of people. As has been noted at various points in this book, the dominant white, male, heterosexual, cisgender, able, middle, and upper-class culture in the United States has been well studied. And for many years, the assumption was that theories based on that subset of society could be broadly applied to all groups without taking into account differences based on power and privilege. However, the limitations of those assumptions are increasingly being revealed (Patton et al. 2016; Reason and Kimball 2012; Taylor 2016).

Future theories are needed to explore the needs and experiences of a more diverse range of learners. A noncomprehensive list of learners to include in the development of future theories include those with disabilities, learners who experience mental-health issues, international students, immigrant and undocumented learners, transgender learners, and learners from a greater range of socioeconomic statuses. As student affairs scholar Kari Taylor (2016) notes, a critical perspective should be applied to current theories that questions the assumptions that have long been normalized by the dominant culture. A key component of thinking more critically about past assumptions is to realize the complexity and overlapping nature of people's identities. Recognizing the importance of intersectionality, or the way that different components of a person's identity, such as having a learning disability and being Latina, results in a nuanced understanding of learners that cannot be categorized by a single identity checkbox. By better acknowledging and exploring the impact of intersectionality on identity, intellectual development, and engagement, the hope is that future theories will be more holistic and will encourage new opportunities for serving learners (Patton et al. 2016).

Another future opportunity for student development theories is to explore how the increasing use of and reliance on digital tools influences learners' intellectual development, sense of identity, and opportunities for engagement (Brown 2016). Developments in this area will be of particular interest to librarians because easy access to information, along with the enormous amount of information now available, influences learners' understanding of authority and evidence. In addition, because of the increased simplicity of sharing information digitally, learners' online identities can be easily (and sometimes unintentionally) shared with a variety of audiences. Learners may develop different abilities over time that influence how they approach the ramifications of digital identity sharing and expectations of privacy. Finally, the social nature of digital platforms also creates evolving expectations about what being involved and engaged in a community looks like. Being part of the digital age has many impacts on learners' behaviors that need to be further explored.

Another area for further exploration is how different types of learning environments impact learners. Most student development theories were created based on observations in residential four-year college or university settings (Taylor 2016). Additional academic settings that could be explored include community colleges, for-profit colleges, and distance-education settings. An increased focus on different academic settings would likely include an examination of the intersections of characteristics such as age, higher variability of socioeconomic status, and veteran experiences. Librarians work in many types of academic settings with a range of learners. An emphasis on differences between these diverse learning environments could help guide future library practices.

As theories are examined to see what changes are needed, a deeper consideration of the role of cultural and historical context is also needed. Just as Perry (1970) observed differences between the cohort he interviewed in the late 1950s and the early 1960s versus the cohort from the early 1970s due to the Vietnam War, more recent historical events also influence learners today. For example, current traditionally aged college graduates are getting married and having children later in life than earlier generations (Settersten 2014). Consequently, many typical behaviors associated with entering adulthood don't happen as soon for this cohort as they did for previous generational cohorts (Settersten, Ottusch, and Schneider 2015). As a result, some of the intellectual and identity development stages may not describe this generational cohort as well as they described past groups. Another example of shifting cultural expectations is the observation that due to Western society's increased focus on wealth and material goods as markers of success, traditional college-aged learners value external validation, such as grades and income, more than they did in the past. Student services providers suggest that this shift from seeking internal to external validation has contributed to an increase in mental-health issues (Eisenberg, Lipson, and Posselt 2016). In addition, this change in source of validation may have implications for intellectual and identity development. The broader cultural and historical context will always influence development. Paying attention to broader trends influencing your learners will help you stay attuned to the theories that best meet their needs.

Finally, some student services scholars believe that learners' development is more fluid and not as well depicted by separate stages (Brown 2016; Patton et al. 2016; Taylor 2016). Most theory developers have acknowledged that the stages of development they suggested were flexible and not meant to represent absolute steps that everyone proceeds through in the same way. Nonetheless, current scholars propose that the challenges of work, school, and family life are even less predictable than may have been previously thought. This shift in thinking doesn't mean that the descriptions of the various stages aren't valuable or insightful but rather means that the boundaries between stages should not be overemphasized.

Final Suggestions for Turning Theory into Practice

Turning theory into actionable work in libraries takes continued work and a persistent awareness of your learners. But it can also be a personally enriching approach to your continued growth as a professional. As has been discussed at various points throughout this book, incorporating theory into practice involves not only knowing what the theories are but also understanding your own context. Robert Reason and Ezekiel Kimball (2012) offer the Theory-to-Practice Model as an insightful way to conceptualize the continued work needed to respond and adapt to a changing environment (see figure 8.1). However, Reason and Kimball also observe that there is no formal route from theory to practice, and each practitioner will develop a path that is meaningful for him or her.

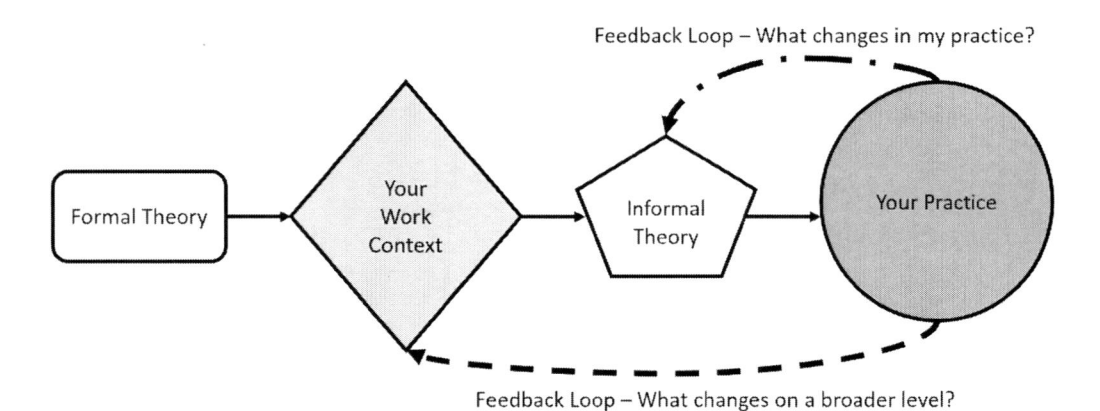

Figure 8.1. Theory-to-Practice Model. *Adapted from Reason and Kimball 2012, 367.*

The Theory-to-Practice Model compares two types of theories: formal and informal. Formal theories are the types of theories that have been discussed throughout much of this book such as the Epistemological Reflection Model or the Student Involvement Theory. Formal theories are research based and typically go through a rigorous review process before they are more broadly accepted by both scholarly and practitioner communities. In contrast, informal theories are much more individual and are informed by specific institutional or local contexts. While informal theories are shaped by an understanding of formal theories, they are intended not to be generalized to someone else's context but instead to adapt as new information about learners or the learners' context is known.

As the Theory-to-Practice Model shows, your specific work context will play a major role in how you determine the informal theories you work with on a day-to-day basis. Another point the Theory-to-Practice Model highlights is that informal theories can be shared by colleagues who work together at the same institution. But you may also have informal theories that primarily guide your own internal compass. Informal theories held by groups or individuals will only adapt to new information if feedback is regularly sought out. The feedback loops in the Theory-to-Practice Model help examine what changes are needed in your individual practice, as well as the changes that may be needed on a broader, programmatic or institutional level.

The final suggestions for incorporating theory into practice explore how to seek out feedback and apply it in individual as well as group contexts. The feedback loops discussed will explore how to collect meaningful assessment information, how to craft personal and programmatic guiding statements, and how to seek out or establish a community of practice to help develop informal theories. Several of these suggestions echo back to ideas raised in chapter 1, which hopefully influenced how you have reflected on the theories presented in this book and will continue to guide your work as a reflective practitioner.

Assessing the Impact of Theories

Actively seeking out assessment data can both inform your individual practice feedback loop and provide programmatic feedback. Unlike other changes you may make in your library such as adding a collection in a new language, changing the hours you are available to accommodate your learners' schedules, or offering a new workshop on an emerging topic, using student development theories to inform your practice won't necessarily give you something to count or specific metrics to evaluate. However, each of the example changes listed above may have come about because of greater attention to particular theories and a willingness to turn observations about your learners into a new personal or programmatic goal. Measuring the increased use of a new service or a collection by tracking attendance or circulation statistics is certainly an appropriate way to evaluate success. But evaluating the success of adapting theories to your local individual and programmatic context will be situational and measured more qualitatively.

Few published studies exist that evaluate theory-based interventions in student affairs work (Patton et al. 2016). While formal evaluations have not been conducted, chapter 1 suggested several individual and group reflective practices that can guide assessment of the impact of theories on your work. In particular, journaling and close listening allow for qualitative insights into the value theories add to your practice.

Journaling or reflective writing is a valuable way to monitor how you are incorporating theories into your individual practice. As noted in chapter 1, if you journal about a particular work setting, such as a class you teach along with the instructional changes you have attempted based on ideas you have gleaned from theories or other sources of inspiration, you will be able to look back at a record of experiences that has changed over time. Reason and Kimball offer specific prompts that you can ask yourself and record responses to as you journal:

- What practices do I frequently use in my work with learners?
- What connections do I make between these practices and my informal theories?
- What evidence do I have that makes me believe these are effective practices? (2012, 370)

If you include your sources of inspiration (including theories), this will give you a reference point for knowing what sources are particularly beneficial for you. This longitudinal record can then be used to assess the impact of the changes you have made and can be useful in writing year-end reports, annual goals, and tenure documents.

You can also use reflective writings from others as a feedback mechanism to help assess the impact of theories on your programmatic work. For example, if your department begins to use reflective writing prompts in instructional settings as a way to conduct formative assessments of learning, you could also evaluate those learning prompts to see how intellectual development changes may be occurring or how different ideas about identity may be emerging across the learners you serve. Discussing these findings as a group, while keeping your institutional context in mind and the diverse learners you work with, can help determine what populations may need more or less assistance and can highlight where your library can have the most impact. Or if colleagues share what they have learned about theories in a professional development workshop, reflective writing prompts to gauge what theories resonate with them and how they have observed development theories in action could be used to shape a departmental or programmatic mission or values statement that reflects the informal theories that emerge.

Closely listening to what is happening in your work environment and with your learner populations was suggested in chapter 1 as a way for knowing when to incorporate theory into practice. Similar to the qualitative data collected through reflective writing, listening to what others have to say (or don't have to say) about new or modified services you or your department try out provides a way to assess how effective the practices you have implemented based on theory really are. On an individual level, recording even informal, unsolicited anecdotes you hear can be an effective way of demonstrating the value you provide to administrators. Depending on how these anecdotes are shared, such as quotes displayed on a website or in a year-end report, consider asking for the learner's permission in order to value their privacy.

A more structured way to listen to your learners and to get programmatic feedback is to hold focus groups. Periodically conducting focus groups can showcase services your learners appreciate as well as concerns they have. Allowing learners to process their thoughts in a group setting can elicit a wider range of feedback and can also prompt some focus group members to remember and share experiences they may not have initially thought were relevant or insightful enough. The information gathered from focus groups or targeted interviews can also be used to refine the way your library thinks about your learner population and what their evolving needs are.

In summary, some qualitative ways to assess how well various theories have influenced your practice include

- reflective writing and
- close listening.

Remember, theories are not recipes or rules you must follow to the letter. Reflect on what you have learned through reflective writing and close listening, and feel free to make adjustments based on what you know about your own practice and context.

Crafting a Guiding Statement

Another way to turn theory into practice is to craft a guiding statement for yourself or your work team based on how you see specific theories applying to both your institutional context and everyday work. Reason and Kimball (2012) describe guiding statements as more flexible interpretations of theories. Guiding statements are a synthesis of the informal theories that guide you and are specific to your local context. Many people draw on implicit ideas to inform their work; as a result, the process of creating a guiding statement can help reveal hidden assumptions and values you may have about yourself, your learners, and your workplace. Periodic refinement and evaluation of your guiding statements provides the opportunity to reflect on the changes needed to help you and your work team to continuously develop in beneficial ways.

Writing a personal guiding statement is another form of reflective writing. Your guiding statement should focus on your personal beliefs as they apply to your work context and the way that you incorporate those beliefs into your everyday practice. However, guiding statements can also be aspirational and can serve as a reminder for the kind of practitioner you strive to be. A common type of guiding statement educators use is a teaching philosophy. A teaching philosophy reflects an individual teacher's guiding beliefs about teaching and learning. Some examples of different teaching philosophies are provided in the box below. These teaching philosophies vary in terms of length, the formality of the language, and in the choice of underlying theories. But each of these teaching philosophies reveals assumptions about what motivates these teaching librarians and their core beliefs.

> **EXAMPLE TEACHING PHILOSOPHIES**
>
> I strive to help our students meet our university's Learning Goals for Graduates by developing their critical-thinking and communication skills, especially as these skills relate to information literacy. Working in partnership with university colleges, departments, and programs, I design online learning tools, create inquiry-based assignments, teach classes and workshops, provide individual research consultations, and develop curricula. In all of these activities, I take a learner-centered approach, incorporating a variety of collaborative and active learning techniques. I respect the knowledge and experience students bring to their research and reinforce the understanding that research is a dynamic, epistemic, and recursive learning process.
> —Hannah Gascho Rempel, Oregon State University, personal communication
>
> I want to redefine the way people think about librarians, inspire as much critical thought as I do laughter, make sure they come away with something they can actually use, and most important, to never, ever, ever bore anyone to tears.
> —Char Booth, California State University, San Marcos, in Booth 2011, 7.
>
> My role is to help create a community of learners who are responsible and responsive to each other as they build on contextual foundations and extend themselves to acquire new knowledge and skills through innovative connections with communities like those they will serve throughout their profession.
> —Loriene Roy, University of Texas, Austin, in Booth 2011, 9.

Library practitioners who focus more on reference or outreach can draw on the teaching philosophy model to reflect on what their core beliefs are and how they want those beliefs to inform the work they do. Guiding statements do not need to be long, but they should be meaningful to you. The most effective guiding statements should be examined on a regular basis and modified based on new theories you have explored or new practices you want to incorporate.

Guiding statements can also be written for programs, departments, or other work teams. The most common forms of guiding statements at a programmatic level are mission and vision statements. Creating a mission statement gives the members of a work team the opportunity to explore what their purpose is and what work they are trying to carry out. Focusing on these key questions involves exploring theoretical frameworks that are meaningful for the group, as well as underlying assumptions that may not have been clearly stated before. A vision statement is intended to be aspirational and to describe the ideal future outcome the group is working toward. Examining mission and vision statements and how they have changed over time can help provide clarity and a renewed sense

Table 8.3. Comparing programmatic guiding statements over time

2011 TEACHING AND ENGAGEMENT DEPARTMENT MISSION	2016 TEACHING AND ENGAGEMENT DEPARTMENT MISSION	SIMILARITIES AND DIFFERENCES
Our mission is to build effective, engaging, and collaborative instruction programs and learning environments by promoting lifelong learning and the education of independent consumers of information.	TED makes the library useful and usable by inspiring enthusiasm for information, learning, and research; by advocating for our users; and by connecting our community members with information in the library and beyond.	*Similarities:* Emphasis on the importance of affect in the learning process through the use of words such as "engaging" and "enthusiasm" *Differences:* The 2011 version focuses more on how learners are directly impacted through experiences in the library, whereas the 2016 version emphasizes librarians' indirect impacts on learning that happen as a result of advocacy.
2011 TEACHING AND ENGAGEMENT DEPARTMENT VISION	**2016 TEACHING AND ENGAGEMENT DEPARTMENT VISION**	**SIMILARITIES AND DIFFERENCES**
Our library is the intersection at which all academic disciplines meet. As such, our educational focus is to partner with faculty to integrate appropriate research skills into the curriculum, provide self-directed learning opportunities, and assist the university community with transferring research into practice.	To build and nurture an inclusive and equitable community of learners who are enthusiastic and curious about exploring information and creating knowledge.	*Similarities:* Emphasis on being active participants in a larger community *Differences:* The 2011 version does not take into account differences between learners that might impact their ability to be self-directed learners, whereas the 2016 version notes that work needs to occur to create an inclusive and equitable learning experience for all learners.

Note

Examples are internal documents from Oregon State University's Teaching and Engagement Department (TED).

of purpose for departments or programs. See table 8.3 for an example of a department's mission and vision statements, and how those statements changed over time.

In summary, guiding statements help reveal

- the core work you do and
- the underlying assumptions, theories, or guiding values for that work.

Guiding statements are most effective when they are

- reviewed regularly and
- treated as a living document.

Once you have written a guiding statement, share the document with others. Seeking out other perspectives can help reveal more underlying assumptions reflected in your work. Input from others can also help surface perceptions about your work, your learners, or your institution that you may not have been able to recognize. The next section discusses how communities of practice can provide broader perspective and support.

Establishing a Community of Practice

A final recommendation for incorporating theories into your practice is to actively engage with a community of librarians or like-minded professionals about questions and challenges you face. A shared way of thinking or a commonly understood framework for solving problems can be a way to bring a community of practice together. Chapter 1 discussed several ways to use theories in groups. Ideally, you could find a group within your own library where you share the same institutional context and goals. However, if you do not have a community or group within your own library, some ways to seek out a community of practice are to look for other people on your campus, in your school district, or in local nonprofit groups who serve a similar population. Many people find community within professional associations, such as the American Library Association, or via regional groups such as statewide school media specialist organizations. If you are able to meet with members of these professional associations regularly either virtually or in person, you can become comfortable discussing issues that concern your practice and trends you observe among your various learner communities. In addition, online communities such as the #critlib Twitter-based group discussed in chapter 1 are increasingly meaningful ways to connect with people who are seeking to explore how their professional ideas and values influence their practice.

Of particular note to academic librarians is the importance of connecting with other people on your campus who work in student affairs or in other student support roles. The challenges students face are often complex and not readily solved by a single unit. For example, Daniel Eisenberg, Sarah Ketchen Lipson, and Julie Posselt (2016), who work with education and public health issues, emphasize that responding to student mental-health issues isn't just the responsibility of student health services; it also requires creating a supportive culture across the whole institution. Students recognize when the larger campus culture creates safe spaces for discussion and are better able to be open about their issues when there is help available in multiple venues. Creating a supportive culture takes a concerted effort across departments and a plan for maintaining clear lines of communication. Librarians who are equipped with the knowledge and language of student development theory are better able to enter these conversations and contribute to creating a supportive culture.

As you engage with your communities of practice, be on the lookout for other theories that help inform the work you do. Now that you have explored student development theories, consider if there are other theories that can guide your interactions with learners or colleagues, or if there are theories that inform how you think about information organization or technology practices. Exercise your curiosity, and keep exploring how your observations mesh with the principles you discover from a wide range of theories.

Key Points

Theories are meant to be used together, not in a stand-alone approach. Regularly gathering feedback at both an individual and institutional level will allow theories to continue to guide your work, even when environmental or societal changes impact your learners. Here are some key points to take away:

- Use multiple theories in an integrative approach when working with learners to value their unique challenges and supports.
- Social science and educational theories are not static but instead continually informed by changing sociocultural factors.
- Seeking feedback through qualitative assessments, by crafting and regularly reviewing guiding statements, and through seeking out discussions with a community will help you incorporate theories into your practice in a meaningful way.

References

Astin, Alexander. 1984. "Student Involvement: A Developmental Theory for Higher Education." *Journal of College Student Personnel* 25 (4): 297–308.

Baxter Magolda, Marcia B. 1992. *Knowing and Reasoning in College: Gender-Related Patterns in Students' Intellectual Development*. Jossey-Bass Higher and Adult Education Series. San Francisco: Jossey-Bass.

———. 2004. "Learning Partnerships Model: A Framework for Promoting Self-Authorship." In *Learning Partnerships: Theory and Models of Practice to Educate for Self-Authorship*, edited by Marcia B. Baxter Magolda and Patricia M. King, 37–62. Sterling, VA: Stylus.

———. 2008. "Three Elements of Self-Authorship." *Journal of College Student Development* 49 (4): 269–84.

Booth, Char. 2011. *Reflective Teaching, Effective Learning: Instructional Literacy for Library Educators*. Chicago: American Library Association.

Brown, Paul Gordon. 2016. "College Student Development in Digital Spaces: College Student Development in Digital Spaces." *New Directions for Student Services* 2016 (155): 59–73.

Chickering, A. W., and Linda Reisser. 1993. *Education and Identity*. 2nd ed. San Francisco: Jossey-Bass.

Eisenberg, Daniel, Sarah Ketchen Lipson, and Julie Posselt. 2016. "Promoting Resilience, Retention, and Mental Health." *New Directions for Student Services* 2016 (156): 87–95.

King, Patricia M., and Karen S. Kitchener. 1994. *Developing Reflective Judgment: Understanding and Promoting Intellectual Growth and Critical Thinking in Adolescents and Adults*. San Francisco: Jossey-Bass.

Patton, Lori D., Kristen A. Renn, Florence Guido-DeBrito, and Stephen John Quaye. 2016. *Student Development in College: Theory, Research, and Practice*. 3rd ed. San Francisco: Jossey-Bass.

Perry, William G. 1970. *Forms of Intellectual and Ethical Development in the College Years: A Scheme*. New York: Holt, Rinehart and Winston.

Reason, Robert D., and Ezekiel W. Kimball. 2012. "A New Theory-to-Practice Model for Student Affairs: Integrating Scholarship, Context, and Reflection." *Journal of Student Affairs Research and Practice* 49 (4): 359–76.

Settersten, Richard. 2014. "Everyone's Freaking Out about Millennials Living at Home. They Shouldn't." *Washington Post*, July 22. http://www.washingtonpost.com/.

Settersten, Richard A., Timothy M. Ottusch, and Barbara Schneider. 2015. "Becoming Adult: Meanings of Markers to Adulthood." In *Emerging Trends in the Social and Behavioral Sciences*, edited by Robert A. Scott and Stephan M. Kosslyn, 1–16. Hoboken, NJ: Wiley.

Taylor, Kari B. 2016. "Diverse and Critical Perspectives on Cognitive Development Theory: Diverse and Critical Perspectives on Cognitive Development Theory." *New Directions for Student Services* 2016 (154): 29–41.

Appendix
Further Recommended Reading

Casas, J. Manuel, Lisa A. Suzuki, Charlene M. Alexander, and Margo A. Jackson, eds. 2016. *Handbook of Multicultural Counseling*. 4th ed. Thousand Oaks, CA: Sage.

Delbanco, A. 2012. *College: What It Was, Is, and Should Be*. Princeton, NJ: Princeton University Press.

Keeling, Richard P., ed. n.d. *Learning Reconsidered: A Campus-Wide Focus on the Student Experience*. Washington, DC: ACPA/NASPA.

Komives, Susan R., John P. Dugan, Julie E. Owen, Craig Slack, Wendy Wagner, and associates. 2011. *The Handbook for Student Leadership Development*. 2nd ed. Hoboken, NJ: Jossey-Bass.

Patton, Lori D., Kristen A. Renn, Florence Guido-DiBrito, and Stephen John Quaye. 2016. *Student Development in College: Theory, Research, and Practice*. 3rd ed. San Francisco: Jossey-Bass.

Peter, Magnolia M., and Marcia B. Baxter Magolda, eds. 2011. *Contested Issues in Student Affairs: Diverse Perspectives and Respectful Dialogue*. Sterling, VA: Stylus.

Pope, Raechele L., Amy L. Reynolds, and John A. Mueller. 2014. *Creating Multicultural Change on Campus*. San Francisco: Jossey-Bass.

Quaye, Stephen John, and Shaun R. Harper, eds. 2014. *Student Engagement in Higher Education: Theoretical Perspectives and Practical Approaches for Diverse Populations*. 2nd ed. New York: Routledge.

Reynolds, Amy L. 2009. *Helping College Students*. San Francisco: Jossey-Bass.

Schuh, John H., Susan R. Jones, and Vasti Torres. 2016. *Student Services: A Handbook for the Profession*. 6th ed. Jossey Bass Higher and Adult Education. San Francisco: Jossey-Bass.

Wilson, Maureen E., Jerlando F. L. Jackson, and Association for the Study of Higher Education. 2011. *College Student Development Theory*. 2nd ed. ASHE Reader Series. Boston: Person Learning Solutions.

Zhang, Naijian, and associates, eds. 2011. *Rentz's Student Affairs Practice in Higher Education*. 4th ed. Springfield, IL: Charles C. Thomas.

Index

Page references for figures are italicized.

ACRL Information Competency Standards, 32
ACRL Information Literacy Framework, 6, 20, 74
Adult Learning Theory, 4–5
assessment, 11, 124
Astin, Alexander, 102–4, 109, 120
authority, 19–23, 27–32, 34, 36, 38, 47
autonomy support, 110

Baxter Magolda, Marcia, 57–60, 68–72, 74, 77, 119

Chickering, Arthur, 80–87, 89–92, 94–95, 98, 120
close listening, 9–*10*, 124–25
College Student Experience Questionnaire, 102–4
community of practice, 128
critlib, 10, 128
CrowdAsk, 73
CSEQ. *See* College Student Experience Questionnaire

Dweck's Theories of Intelligence, 5–6

Epistemological Reflection Model, 55–65, *118*–19
Erikson, Erik, 80–*81*

Four Ways of Knowing, 57, 59, 69–70, 119. *See also* Epistemological Reflection Model
free-choice learning, 110, *112*
Freud, Sigmund, 80

Generation Open, 98
guiding statements, 125–27

Head, Alison, 77
high impact practices, 106–8, *117*, 120
HIPS. *See* high impact practices

IDP. *See* individual development plan
ill-structured problems, 44–49, 51, *117*–18
individual development plan, 75–76
instructional techniques: Cephalonian method, *33*–34; mind map, *33*, 37; minute paper, 34, 97; misconception/preconception check, *33*, 36; muddiest point , *33*–34
integrative approach, 13, 116
Intellectual and Ethical Development Theory, 21–38; dualism, 22–23, 26–*29*, 32–35, 38, 43, 116–*17*; multiplicity, 22–23, 26, *28*–30, 33–36, 38, 43, 116–*17*; relativism, 22–23, 26, *28*–*29*, 30–31, *33*, 36–38, 43, 116–*17*
intersectionality, 91, 121

journaling. *See* reflective writing

K–12 engagement, 109–10
Kegan, Robert, 69
King, Patricia, 43–45, 118
Kitchener, Karen, 43–45, 118

Learning Partnerships Model, 68, 70–74, 76, *117*–20
Library Anxiety Theory, 1, 4–6, *8*, *12*, 85–86

mission statements, 126
motivational interviewing, 88

National Survey of Student Engagement, 14, 103–6
NSSE. *See* National Survey of Student Engagement

outreach activities: citizen science, 51–52; Crafternoon, 38; displays, 38, 85–86, 90, 98; DIY bike repair, 76; Human Library, 65; maker faire, 38; speed friending, *89*, 108; TEDx, 76

peer education programs, *83*–84, 97
peer reference services, 73, *83*, 97
Perry, William, 21, 24–25, 116
persistence, student, 103, 106, *117*, 120
Project Information Literacy, 46, 51, 71

reasoning patterns, gender based, 57–59
Reflective Judgment Model, 42–46, 48–49, 51, 117–19; prereflective thinking, 43, *117*–18; quasi-reflective thinking, 43, 117–18; reflective thinking, 43, 117–18
reflective listening, 73, *88, 90, 96*
reflective practices, *9*–11, 124–25
reflective reading, 9
reflective writing, 8–11, 124–25
Reisser, Linda, 80–87, 89–92, 94–95, 98, 120

self-authoring, 69, 71–72
Seven Vectors of Individual Development, 80–82, 94–95, 97–98, 120; autonomy toward interdependence, 86–88, *117*, 120; developing competence, 82–84, *117*, 120; developing integrity, 94, *117*; developing purpose, 92–94, *117*; establishing identity, 90–92, *117*; managing emotions, 84–86, *117*, 120 mature interpersonal relationships, 88–90, *117*, 120
Social Development Theory, 72
Student Engagement, 101–6, 109–10
Student Involvement Theory, 102–3, *117*–18, 120–21
student populations: first-year undergraduates, 44, 57, *107*; graduate students, 31, 45, 50–51, 75; historically underrepresented students, 71, 108, 110; international students, *8*, 12, 89, 121; K–12 students, 56, 118, 125–126; upper-division undergraduates, *45*

teaching philosophies, 125–26
theory development, 3–4
theory use, 4–7
Theory-to-Practice Model, 123
tutoring techniques, 60–62

vision statements, 126–27
Vygotsky, Lev, 72

Wikipedia, 26, 32, 74–76

About the Authors

Hannah Gascho Rempel is associate professor at Oregon State University Libraries in the Teaching and Engagement Department. Since joining OSU in 2007, she has spearheaded the development of OSU Libraries' services for graduate students and has been deeply involved in the Teaching and Engagement Department's transition to a more strategic focus on learner-centered instruction activities. She has published on how undergraduate research behaviors are impacted by student development theories in the journal *portal: Libraries and the Academy*. Her presentations at LOEX, Library Instruction West, and to her own university community have focused on undergraduate research behaviors and curiosity with an emphasis on the importance of considering student development stages. In addition she writes frequently on providing library services targeted at graduate students' needs. She helps shape the conversation about user needs and web use in libraries by editing the peer-reviewed publication the *Journal of Web Librarianship*.

Kelly McElroy is assistant professor and student engagement and community outreach librarian at Oregon State University Libraries. Her research focuses on student engagement and critical pedagogy in library instruction. She is the coeditor of the two-volume book *Critical Library Pedagogy Handbook*, which won the 2017 ACRL Instruction Section Rockman Publication of the Year Award. Forthcoming publications examine how libraries create spaces for student voices and ways for librarians to collaborate with instructors in developing innovative assignments.

Laurie M. Bridges is associate professor and instruction and outreach librarian at Oregon State University Libraries. In addition to her MLIS, Bridges holds an MS in college student services administration; her master's thesis explored the relationship between self-esteem and student engagement within the framework of student development and feminist theories. In addition to her role within the libraries, Bridges has served for over five years as a graduate advisor and thesis committee chair for numerous students in the OSU College Student Services Administration program. Her recent publications and presentations have focused on student engagement with libraries.